The Inside Players:
Master the Manifestation Game

Rachel Christensen

Copyright © 2025 Rachel Christensen
All rights reserved.

No part of this book may be reproduced, distributed, or transmitted in any form or by any means, including photocopying, recording, or other electronic or mechanical methods, without the prior written permission of the author, except in the case of brief quotations embodied in critical reviews and certain other non-commercial uses permitted by copyright law.

ISBN: 978-0-473-73363-6

Published by Rachel Christensen
Auckland, New Zealand
www.rachelchristensenofficial.com

First Edition: January 2025

Edited by Paul Mayhew
Illustrations by Kayla Christensen, Fine Artist, New Zealand

Disclaimer: This book is intended for informational purposes only and does not constitute professional advice. Readers are encouraged to consult with a qualified professional for personal guidance.

Acknowledgements

To my parents: I hold deep respect for the paths you walked and for the ancestors who came before me. My mum's survival through unimaginable horrors is a testament to the power of endurance and resilience.

I honour you, not only for the gifts you passed down but also for the painful secrets you carry. They have taught me invaluable lessons about courage, healing, and growth. Without your struggles and sacrifices, I would not be here to share these stories or explore these truths.

Growth and success are never achieved in isolation. They arise through the grace of those who walk with us—our teachers, guides, allies, and the lessons life brings. I owe a profound debt of appreciation and gratitude to my teacher, Myree, for her guidance and wisdom on this journey.

To my husband, Luke, your unwavering belief in me and your constant encouragement throughout my evolution has been the greatest source of support. Without you, this book would not have been possible.

To everyone who has played a role in my journey, I thank you. It is with immense humility that I offer this book—a reflection of the many hands, hearts, and experiences that have brought me here. May it inspire others to embrace their own journey of healing, transformation, and creation.

Contents

Acknowledgements iii

Introduction 1

Sacred Feminine Archetypes: The Inward Journey 17

Chapter 1 – The Maiden Archetype: The Visionary Dreamer 19

Chapter 2 – The Lover Archetype: The Passionate Embodier 31

Chapter 3 – The Mother Archetype: The Sacred Container 45

Chapter 4 – The Huntress Archetype: The Truth Seeker 59

Chapter 5 – The Healer Archetype: The Inner Transformer 73

Chapter 6 – The Queen Archetype: The Worthy Receiver 87

Chapter 7 – The Wild Woman Archetype: The Authentic Liberator 99

Sacred Masculine Archetypes: Moving into Action 111

Chapter 8 – The King Archetype: The Powerful Leader 113

Chapter 9 – The Magician Archetype: The Quantum Jumper 129

Chapter 10 – The Sage Archetype: The Universal Guide 141

Chapter 11 – Manifestation Practices 155

Putting it all Together: Embodying Surrendered Manifestation 161

Stay Connected 165

Introduction

"What you think, you become. What you feel, you attract. What you imagine, you create."

—*Buddha*

My Turning Point from Control to Surrender

I grew up in Perth, Australia, the youngest of three children. My mum came from a large, impoverished family in Malaysia and had a difficult childhood. She met my dad, an Australian when he was working in Malaysia, and they eventually settled in Perth. His job took him away often, leaving her to manage the household alone and isolated from her family.

Our home was a chaotic environment with a constant sense of unpredictability. This meant my siblings and I had to grow up quickly, learning to stay hyper-aware to prevent things from spiralling out of control.

Mum's childhood trauma weighed heavily on her, and the scars of extreme poverty and abuse often overwhelmed her. A vivid example is how, when recovering from a broken leg, she began manically hacking at her cast with a butcher's knife to free herself from the discomfort. I was terrified she might slip and embed the knife in her thigh. Even so, I set aside my fear and focused on de-escalating the situation, a familiar role by then.

Many situations forced us to handle things beyond our years, like dealing with a boyfriend who became abusive when he

Introduction

drank. At fourteen, during a layover in Singapore, he began attacking mum in our hotel room whilst she collapsed into a frozen, childlike state. I instinctively stepped in to shield her, matching his energy and daring him to hit me instead.

It was my way of deflecting his anger and challenging his power. I didn't care what might happen to me. He began spitting on me, calling me a whore, then stormed off into the night. He was remorseful the next day, ashamed as always. As was the pattern, we just carried on as though nothing had happened.

These experiences were the backdrop of my childhood, leaving me desensitised. I learned to compartmentalise and keep moving forward without dwelling on stuff—knowing that things could change in an instant.

In my early twenties, I discovered what felt like a lifeline. I came across mainstream personal development frameworks, and for the first time in my life, I felt I could shape my own reality—a way to bring order to the chaos. Without clear guidance, I latched onto the belief that hard work and discipline could provide the stability I had always sought.

I taught myself that the key to controlling my circumstances was to push harder. And for a while, it worked! Each success only reinforced my conviction, and this belief became the cornerstone of my life. I immersed myself in self-help books on mindset and goal setting, breaking down my ambitions into milestones.

Despite my efforts, after a few years, something felt fundamentally wrong. A key moment of realisation was when I was sitting in my office, going through the motions like a robot—putting in the hours, hustling, and following society's rules of 'success.' This was supposed to be what creating success looked like, yet I felt empty; my body was there, but my mind felt trapped, and my soul felt like it was slipping away. A growing disconnect gnawed at me, a quiet voice whispering that something essential was missing.

Red flags often surfaced at work, but I ignored them, clinging to resilience and control, convinced they'd lead to the breakthrough I sought. This dynamic continued until a situation made it undeniably clear that I'd been manipulated by people I trusted (more on this later). It was a painful but necessary wake-up call.

Following this, life slowed down, and I finally had space to reflect. I began questioning everything—my choices, beliefs, and the boundaries I'd been willing to ignore. Growing up, I survived by focusing on people's positive aspects. This coping mechanism of excessive 'positive reframing' followed me into adulthood, leaving me unsure when to walk away as it blurred the line between acceptable and harmful treatment.

My chaotic early years left me without a true sense of stability. So, I sought it externally, placing too much trust in workplaces, bosses, and formulas for success because I didn't know how to rely on myself. I believed that if I worked hard enough, I'd finally find the security I craved. Inevitably, this reliance on external validation left me vulnerable, creating blind spots and leading to poor choices. These unconscious habits became a form of self-sabotage, keeping me stuck in a cycle that trapped me in the very chaos I was trying to escape.

During this transition period, I was drawn to holistic healing and spiritual practices, which sparked a profound shift within me. I began to move away from seeking external solutions and instead focused on reconnecting with my inner voice.

"As I deepened into my awakening, I uncovered a powerful truth: I had never truly felt safe 'letting go.'"

Introduction

I had clung to control for years, convinced it was the only way to feel safe in an unpredictable world. Letting go of old fears and deeply ingrained beliefs wasn't easy, but each release brought a newfound sense of freedom. Slowly, I recognised that control wasn't protecting me—on the contrary, it was keeping me stuck.

During this time, I discovered that surrender wasn't about giving up but about trusting myself to navigate life's flow. As I embraced this shift, my relentless drive softened, replaced by a sense of ease I hadn't experienced before. Opportunities and relationships began to align effortlessly. What once felt like a constant struggle started to flow naturally—life was happening for me, not to me.

I came to a pivotal realisation that my approach to manifestation had been rooted in forcing outcomes. I was so focused on controlling the external world that I'd ignored the internal alignment necessary for true transformation. The answer wasn't outside me; it was within.

This understanding didn't just change how I manifest—it changed how I live. And it's the foundation of this book: aligning with what already exists within, reconnecting to the truths we've always carried, and embracing life as a co-creative partner. This is the journey of becoming—a process of remembering who we truly are and allowing life to flow through us with grace.

This journey from control to surrender is not just mine; it reflects a universal truth about how we relate to our inner and outer worlds. We all carry hopes and dreams of something greater—a life filled with freedom, possibility, and fulfilment. These dreams are the quiet whispers of our potential, calling us to step into something bigger and more meaningful. But too often, the reality we experience feels disconnected from those dreams. Instead of ease and flow, we find ourselves weighed down by the challenges of daily life, caught in a cycle where progress feels slow or unattainable.

For many of us, life feels like a series of struggles…

Manifestation is the process of bringing our desires, dreams, and goals into reality. This requires more than just 'action' or sheer effort; it is a process of transformation based on harmony between our inner state—our beliefs, emotions, and subconscious patterns—and the outer world we experience. Only when we can nurture this alignment can we bridge our dreams with reality.

Effortless manifestation emerges when intention, inner harmony, and aligned action come together, forming a collaborative partnership with the universe.

Manifestation that feels difficult or stagnant is often a sign of internal resistance rooted in emotional patterns, beliefs, or past traumas. These blocks may arise from personal experiences, societal conditioning, or inherited ancestral patterns. This resistance is often part of an evolutionary mechanism deeply wired within us to protect us from *perceived* risks. Over thousands of years, our subconscious evolved to prioritise safety above all else. Any kind of change—even one we deeply desire—can trigger these protective mechanisms, creating an internal conflict between the life we want and the patterns we've relied on to survive.

While these mechanisms once played a vital role in ensuring survival during moments of real danger or life-threatening situations, they often persist in ways that no longer serve us in modern society. This lingering resistance manifests as misalignment or self-sabotaging behaviours, shaping how we perceive the world and how we respond to opportunities. Consider it like carrying armour we no longer need, weighing us down and blocking us from fully embracing the life we seek.

Scan the QR code to deepen your understanding of manifestation.

Healing these patterns is essential to transforming our internal landscape. By recognising and processing these blocks, we allow ourselves to move beyond survival mode and reconnect with the present moment and our true potential. This process creates the clarity and harmony needed for manifestation to flow effortlessly, opening the door to a life that reflects our deepest dreams and aspirations.

Balancing Masculine and Feminine Energies

Ancient philosophies like Taoism and Hinduism teach that true harmony is achieved by integrating *yin* (feminine/being) and *yang* (masculine/doing) energies. These forces represent the dualistic aspects of life—light and dark, rest and movement, receptivity and action—forming a balanced flow that allows all aspects of existence to thrive.

In the context of manifestation, **Sacred Feminine** energy (*yin*) represents the womb of creation. It is fluid, intuitive, receptive, and present, allowing a protective space for dreams to form and grow. This initiates the process by inviting us to surrender control, trust and co-create with the flow of the universe.

Sacred Masculine energy (*yang*), on the other hand, provides the structure (including a linear sense of time that focuses on the future or past), intellect, discipline, and action needed to transform the inner alignment of the Sacred Feminine into tangible results.

Together, these energies form a balanced rhythm that mirrors the natural cycles of life to bring dreams into reality.

Thus, true manifestation begins with the Sacred Feminine. Our dreams, shaped by our thoughts, emotions, and energy, originate in the imagination and subconscious mind. By first cultivating harmony and alignment within, we create the conditions for our external reality to reflect this balance. Once this foundation is established, the Sacred Masculine steps in, translating the dream into purposeful action. Without this initial inner alignment, action often feels forced, and progress becomes a struggle.

Over centuries, Western religious and industrial culture has emphasised hard work, discipline, and productivity as the primary route to success. This has conditioned us to prioritise the external effort to control (or *manufacture*) outcomes over the inner work needed for true alignment. Such **action-oriented manifestation** draws on the **will centre** located in the solar plexus, also known as the *Manipura chakra* in Hindu and Buddhist traditions.

Governing willpower, personal power, and the drive to act, this energy system embodies ambition and self-discipline. While these qualities are essential, ancient teachings emphasise balance across all chakras, and their overemphasis in today's fast-paced and results-driven society often leads to imbalance and burnout.

This imbalance between the Sacred Masculine and Sacred Feminine glorifies visible achievements at the expense of inner balance, creating a cycle of endless 'hustling' with little meaningful progress. Since our external reality mirrors our inner state, forcing outcomes without alignment disrupts the natural flow of manifestation and leads to resistance rather than ease.

To address these cultural biases, this book is grounded in the **Sacred Feminine Manifestation Method**—a pathway to restoring balance and manifesting with greater trust and ease.

The Law of Resonance

The basis of manifestation is that our inner state shapes our outer reality. This concept reflects the **Law of Attraction**, which suggests that by focusing on positive or negative thoughts, we attract corresponding outcomes. This law has gained wide recognition in recent years, particularly in popular books like *The Secret* by Rhonda Byrne.

The **Law of Resonance** expands on this by highlighting that it's not just our thoughts but our entire vibrational state that shapes reality. 'Vibration' refers to the energy we emit through our thoughts, emotions, and beliefs. Each emotion and belief resonates at a unique frequency, forming the energy we project into the world. This energy influences how we interact with life and determines what we attract, as 'like attracts like' in experiences, people, and opportunities.

Essentially, the energy we resonate with dictates the reality we create, emphasising the importance of aligning our inner state with desired outcomes. This realisation shifts our focus beyond mental energy to a more holistic view of our state of being. Manifestation isn't only about taking action; it's about *becoming*.

If this all seems too unscientific and 'woo-woo,' consider that the **wave-particle duality** principle of quantum mechanics states that everything in the universe is fundamentally composed of energy. Physics teaches us that all matter, including every atom and cell in our body, vibrates at different frequencies. Even the smallest particles of matter are in constant motion, radiating energy.

While physics primarily addresses the physical realm, emerging research in fields like neuroscience and psychophysiology bridges the gap between the physical and emotional. For example, our emotions and thoughts generate measurable electromagnetic fields, particularly in the brain and heart, as shown in studies by institutions like the HeartMath Institute. These fields interact with the energy around us, aligning with the concept that our inner vibrational state shapes the outer experiences we attract—an idea central to the **Law of Resonance**.

> *"The universe does not respond to what we want, but to who we are. When we vibrate at the frequencies of abundance, joy, and love, we naturally create experiences that mirror those feelings."*

The Law of Resonance suggests that the energy we emit through our thoughts, emotions, and beliefs vibrates at specific frequencies, influencing the energy of the world around us, like tuning forks vibrating at the same frequency. Quantum mechanics further supports the idea that observer interaction—including intention—can alter outcomes, as seen in experiments like the double-slit experiment.

This experiment showed that particles behave differently depending on whether they are being observed, highlighting the profound impact of consciousness on physical reality. Principles such as these suggest a scientific framework that helps us understand how inner alignment with emotions like love and gratitude can create a resonance that manifests experiences matching those frequencies.

To manifest effectively, we must align our entire being—thoughts, emotions, and beliefs—with the energy of what we desire. This is the basis of our limitless potential as powerful co-creators of our reality.

Whilst the principles of manifestation are universal, each person's path is unique and shaped by individual desires, experiences, beliefs, and subconscious patterns.

The Dual Nature of Resonance

The Law of Resonance has a **dual nature**, meaning it operates on both the conscious and subconscious levels. While we may consciously set clear intentions and take purposeful action externally, the hidden patterns in our subconscious exert the strongest influence over our energy. These can function as fragmented, **internalised defences**—adaptive mechanisms that were developed to protect us but are now creating barriers to conscious growth. They form blind spots that distort our energy field, requiring deep self-awareness to uncover and release.

Imagine looking at an object underwater. The image appears warped because the water refracts light, altering our perception of the object's true form. Similarly, subconscious patterns ripple through our energy, distorting the signals we emit, perceive, and receive. These distortions prevent us from achieving alignment with our desires, much like how a warped image underwater obscures clarity. To manifest effectively, we must identify and clear these subconscious distortions, allowing our energy to resonate clearly with what we wish to attract.

In the early 20th century, Swiss psychologist Carl Jung introduced the concept of **individuation**, the process of becoming whole by uncovering and integrating the fragmented parts of ourselves. Jung's thoughts on this have been commonly paraphrased as, "Until you make the unconscious conscious, it will direct your life, and you will call it fate." This highlights the importance of bringing hidden beliefs into awareness to release distortions and realign with our true intentions.

When our conscious and subconscious energies are in harmony, our vibrational state becomes clear and coherent. This clarity naturally attracts the people, opportunities, and experiences that resonate with our desires, allowing the manifestation to unfold effortlessly.

> *"True manifestation is about aligning with your deepest truths and creating a space where effort and ease coexist."*

To navigate these subconscious distortions and achieve alignment, we need a framework for understanding and transforming resistance.

Manifestation Blocks, Obstacles, and Shadows

Resistance in the manifestation process can be understood through three interconnected elements: blocks, obstacles, and shadows. Together, they form the foundation for uncovering and transforming misalignment.

MANIFESTATION BLOCK QUIZ

Manifestation Blocks

Blocks are overarching categories of resistance that disrupt the alignment needed for creation. They represent where our energy is misaligned, often falling into one of three categories:

- **Abundance Blocks** (*The Block to Receiving*): Challenges rooted in scarcity beliefs or feelings of unworthiness.
- **Expansion Blocks** (*The Block to Growth*): Resistance tied to fears of responsibility or the inability to contain growth.
- **Alignment Blocks** (*The Block to Truth*): Misalignment between our goals and our soul's deeper desires.

Obstacles

Obstacles are tangible or intangible signals that reveal where blocks exist. They manifest as self-sabotage, recurring setbacks, or emotional resistance. These obstacles are symptoms, pointing to the deeper shadows that anchor resistance.

Shadows

Shadows are the root causes of resistance. These hidden fears, inherited beliefs, or unresolved emotions distort our energy and create misalignment. Shadows are not barriers to be avoided; they are opportunities for transformation. By confronting them, we can uncover the hidden gifts within.

To address these layers of resistance, we turn to archetypes. These universal patterns serve as tools for navigating and transforming misalignment.

Archetypes of Manifestation

Throughout history, myth and storytelling have provided tools for understanding the human psyche. Jung introduced the concept of **archetypes** as universal patterns within the collective unconscious, reflecting shared experiences that transcend time and culture. These archetypes illuminate the hidden layers of consciousness, subtly shaping how we perceive and interact with the world.

In this book, archetypes are presented as the blueprint for recognising and navigating manifestation blocks. Each archetype reflects both light ('gift') and dark ('shadow') aspects of the self:

- **Gifts** represent healthy expressions of the archetype, strengths, and wisdom that foster alignment and growth.
- **Shadows** arise from the archetype's unhealthy expressions, unexamined beliefs, traits, or emotions that create internal resistance and manifest as external obstacles.

Paradoxically, shadows hold the potential to reveal our greatest strengths. This is because working with archetypes uncovers the gifts hidden within our shadows, revealing both our strengths and areas for growth. Such processing helps us move past resistance, fostering clarity, flow, and resonance in manifestation. Be aware that this work takes compassion, curiosity, and courage, but the reward is *transformative*: unlocking the power to consciously create a life of resonance and fulfilment.

Transforming Shadows into Gifts

Recognising shadows as the root cause of manifestation blocks transmutes them into powerful catalysts for transformation. This transformative process follows three key steps:

1. **Identify the Block**: Determine whether the resistance stems from abundance, expansion, or alignment challenges.
2. **Recognise the Obstacle**: Observe recurring signals of resistance in your life—patterns that point to internal shadows.
3. **Transform the Shadow**: Use archetypes as tools to address the root cause, uncover hidden gifts, and restore alignment.

Jung's archetypal shadow work provides a roadmap for this inner exploration. By confronting and integrating subconscious patterns, we transform limiting beliefs, align more fully with our truest selves, and create a vibrational field that resonates with our desires.

Sacred Feminine and Masculine Archetypes

The archetypes explored in this book are divided into **Sacred Feminine** and **Sacred Masculine** energies, each serving distinct but complementary roles. The Sacred Masculine archetypes typically correspond to action, while Sacred Feminine archetypes are connected to inner processes and reflection (**Table 1**).

Table 1 Sacred Feminine and Sacred Masculine archetypes.

Sacred Feminine Archetypes	Sacred Masculine Archetypes
The Maiden	The King
The Lover	The Magician
The Mother	The Sage
The Huntress	
The Healer	
The Queen	
The Wild Woman	

Together, they teach us the art of balancing our inner work with external action, guiding us to recognise when to act, reflect, and let go. This is why they form the framework for this book.

The Fluidity of Archetypes

While archetypes provide a flexible framework, manifestation is not a linear path. Each archetype represents unique energies that adapt to different stages of your journey. Some archetypes, like the Maiden, offer a clear framework for identifying obstacles, understanding the shadows, and transforming them into gifts (obstacle > shadow > gift). These types of archetypes offer a relatively defined path, guiding us through the inner dynamics that shape manifestation.

In contrast, archetypes like the Huntress or Healer demand deeper exploration. Their challenges often appear as emotional, energetic, or psychological shifts that unfold gradually. These archetypes invite introspection and inner work to encourage transformation to arise naturally over time.

The beauty of archetypes lies in their adaptability. They evolve with you, serving as flexible tools for growth and alignment. While certain archetypes may resonate strongly at specific moments, others will surface later when their wisdom is most needed.

Manifestation is deeply personal. Although archetypes provide a map, the journey is yours to navigate. Each one honours your unique rhythm, guiding you toward intentional creation and authentic alignment.

Throughout the book, I will share parts of my personal journey to illustrate how the steps of manifestation are reflected through the lens of archetypes, transforming not only what we achieve but how we engage with the world and ourselves.

In the next section, we'll explore the Sacred Feminine archetypes, which guide us inward, helping us cultivate the energy of *being* rather than doing. This inward focus forms the foundation upon which aligned action of the Sacred Masculine can develop.

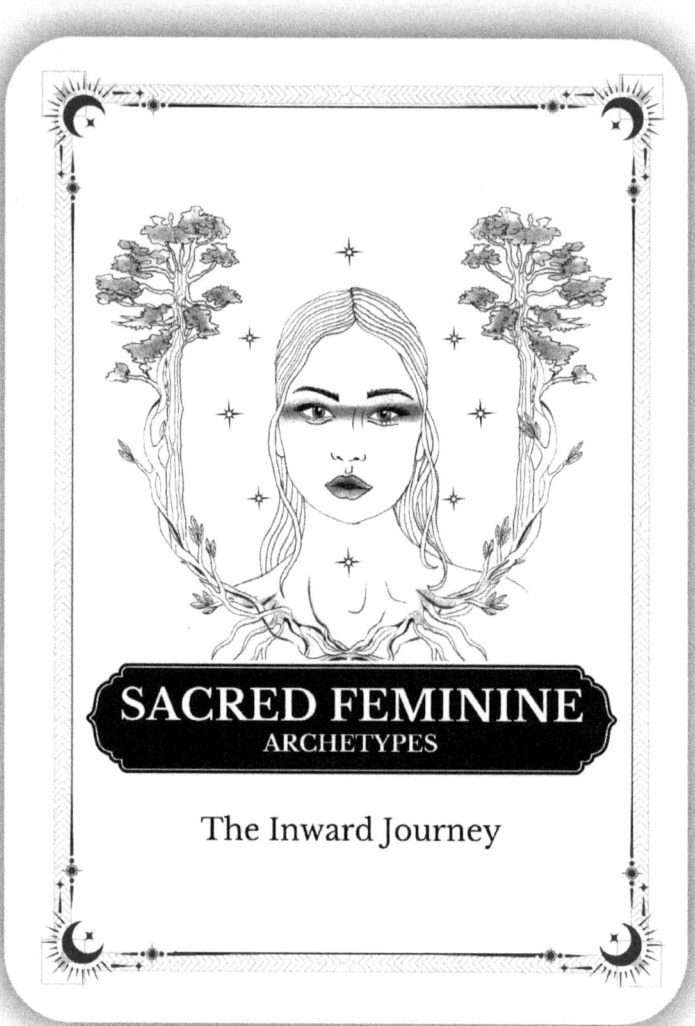

Sacred Feminine Archetypes: The Inward Journey

The following chapters summarise the Sacred Feminine archetypes:

- The Maiden
- The Lover
- The Mother
- The Huntress
- The Healer
- The Queen
- The Wild Woman

These deal primarily with internal processes like dreaming, nurturing, emotional alignment, and clearing blocks; their role focuses on the inner work that sets the solid foundation for manifestation.

CHAPTER 1
The Maiden Archetype: The Visionary Dreamer

"Dreams are the seedlings of reality."
—James Allen

THE MAIDEN BEGINS the manifestation journey, inviting us to dream without limitations and explore our true desires.

This is the 'dreaming phase,' where we cast our net wide to reach as far as possible, like a rocket exploring vast, uncharted realms. We think without practical constraints, allowing our aspirations to expand freely and discover what is untapped within. The Maiden's energy reconnects us with curiosity and childlike wonder, inspiring us to boldly pursue our truest desires, embrace creativity, and envision possibilities beyond our current reality, cultivating dreams that are yet to take shape.

When we resist the Maiden's influence, our dreams remain limited by what feels safe or practical, stifling growth and potential. This self-limitation may lead us to settle for less than we truly desire, keeping us grounded in fear or familiarity and disconnected from deeper aspirations.

Chapter 1 – The Maiden Archetype: The Visionary Dreamer

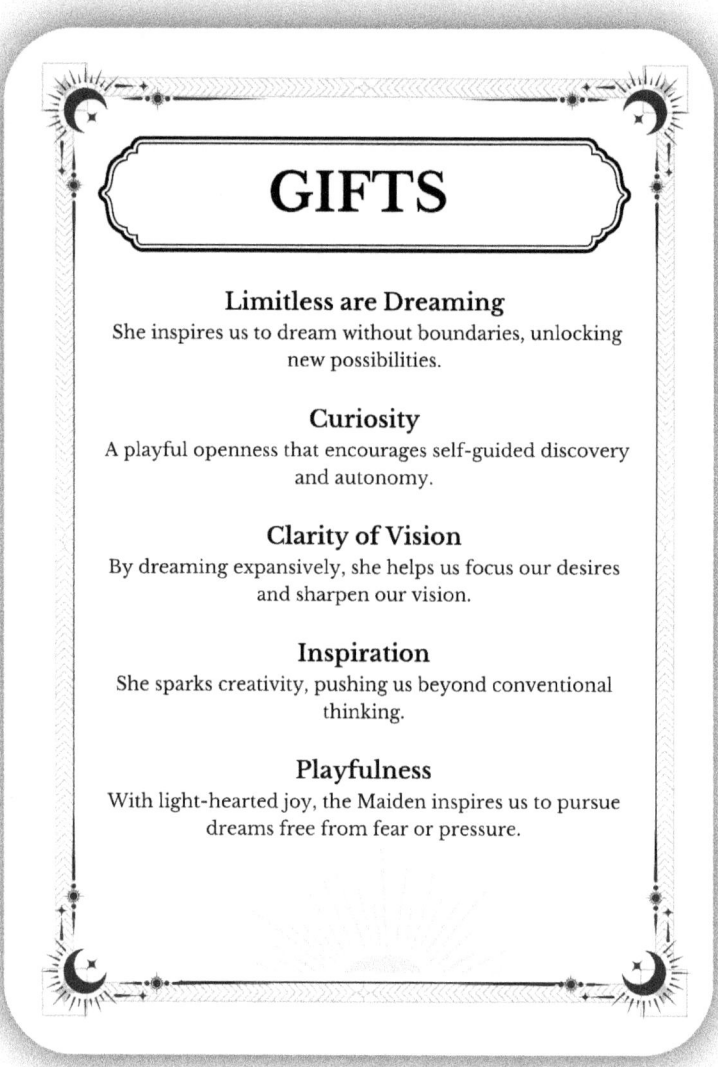

GIFTS

Limitless are Dreaming
She inspires us to dream without boundaries, unlocking new possibilities.

Curiosity
A playful openness that encourages self-guided discovery and autonomy.

Clarity of Vision
By dreaming expansively, she helps us focus our desires and sharpen our vision.

Inspiration
She sparks creativity, pushing us beyond conventional thinking.

Playfulness
With light-hearted joy, the Maiden inspires us to pursue dreams free from fear or pressure.

The dreamer who dares to step forward finds the path beneath their feet.

The Inside Players: Master the Manifestation Game

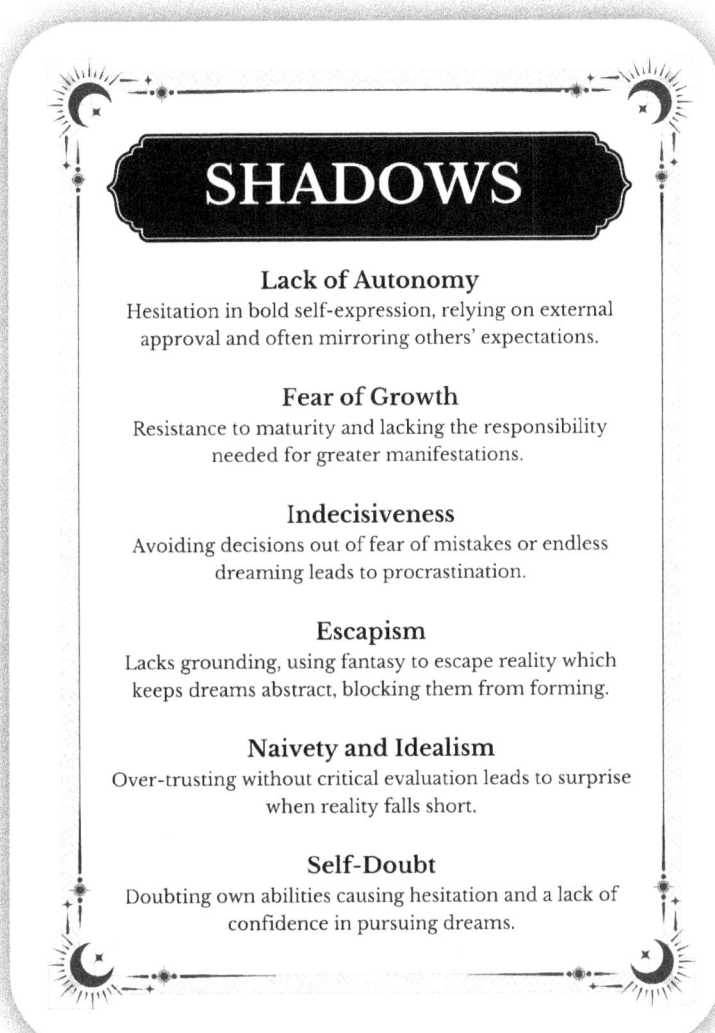

SHADOWS

Lack of Autonomy
Hesitation in bold self-expression, relying on external approval and often mirroring others' expectations.

Fear of Growth
Resistance to maturity and lacking the responsibility needed for greater manifestations.

Indecisiveness
Avoiding decisions out of fear of mistakes or endless dreaming leads to procrastination.

Escapism
Lacks grounding, using fantasy to escape reality which keeps dreams abstract, blocking them from forming.

Naivety and Idealism
Over-trusting without critical evaluation leads to surprise when reality falls short.

Self-Doubt
Doubting own abilities causing hesitation and a lack of confidence in pursuing dreams.

A vision untethered drifts forever; without courage, dreams remain whispers in the wind.

Chapter 1 – The Maiden Archetype: The Visionary Dreamer

Overcoming the Obstacles of the Maiden

The obstacles of this archetype often arise from the overwhelming options of limitless potential. Without a clear sense of direction or autonomy, the Maiden may remain stuck in endless dreaming, fearful of taking bold steps or committing to a vision. This lack of grounding prevents her from manifesting her dreams into reality.

Embracing the Beginner's Mind

A key challenge in the Maiden phase is the irresistible urge to know precisely *how* and *when* our dreams will come to life. While asking questions is a natural part of curiosity, fixating on specifics can tether us to practicality, narrowing the Maiden's boundless freedom to explore without constraint. This craving for certainty can shift from exploration into rigidity, like building walls around our vision and trapping it within the borders of what feels predictable. Instead of welcoming the thrill of uncharted possibilities, we risk stifling the expansive nature of our dreams.

The Maiden's power lies in her limitless imagination, where dreams emerge freely, unbounded by judgment or constraint. Yet, this phase also comes with the struggle to ground these visions in actionable clarity. This stage is about embracing curiosity as a gateway to discernment. And her role is to open the floodgates of possibility, allowing every dream to take shape without prematurely narrowing its potential.

The **beginner's mind** offers a liberating shift—a fresh way of seeing that invites us to look at each vision without boundaries or expectations. Embracing this mindset releases the need for rigid answers or fixed timelines, allowing space for our dreams to flourish in their own way. With the beginner's mind, every possibility becomes an open canvas, free from the weight of past assumptions or fears of falling short. This openness rekindles our curiosity, reconnects us with the present moment, and invites us to let the journey unfold with limitless potential.

Dreaming Boldly Without Limits

Shaped by societal expectations and past conditioning, many of us carry a fear of 'dreaming too big.' Over time, we internalise what's deemed 'realistic' or 'acceptable' and confine our aspirations to familiar, safe limits. This self-imposed restraint often reflects a deep-seated need for security and validation, urging us to seek external affirmation and leading to people-pleasing behaviour rather than trust in our own vision.

Attachment theory sheds some light on this. For those with insecure attachment styles, for example, early childhood relationships with caregivers often tie self-worth to external approval, making bold dreams feel risky or even unattainable. In such cases, self-censorship becomes a form of self-protection. Dreaming boldly invites us to break free from restrictive norms and pursue what feels true to our grandest desires, even if it seems beyond reach.

> *"The courage to dream without limits empowers us to envision a reality that transcends traditional boundaries, reconnecting us with our innate potential."*

To overcome this, we must cultivate the courage to validate our own aspirations, daring to believe in our most expansive dreams despite societal pressures or past disappointments. This is the essence of dreaming big: embracing the audacity to trust our grandest visions and believe that what we imagine is truly within reach.

Dreaming with Purpose

While the Maiden encourages us to dream freely, there is a risk of getting lost in fantasy—especially since dreaming can become a form of **escapism**, allowing us to retreat into abstract possibilities to avoid life's challenges. This is particularly common among individuals who experienced childhood trauma or instability, where fantasy provided a safe escape from difficult or painful realities.

Chapter 1 – The Maiden Archetype: The Visionary Dreamer

When the external world feels unsafe or uncontrollable, an idealised internal fantasy world can soothe and offer a sense of control. However, as we grow, this can develop into an adult coping mechanism and keep us stuck in an ungrounded space, preventing us from taking action toward our desires.

While dreaming is essential to the manifestation process, it must be balanced with grounded steps and anchored in a meaningful 'why?' Having a clear purpose behind our dreams helps us stay rooted and motivated, connecting our visions to a deeper, more resilient foundation. The key is to recognise the difference between dreaming as an emotional escape rather than a productive visioning process.

Balancing Big Dreams in Manageable Doses

Setting unrealistic aspirations from the start may set us up for failure before we have even begun. This kind of resistance acts as a 'protection mechanism' that holds us back from true progress by shielding us from potential disappointment, feelings of inadequacy, or even a fear of growth. For some, the prospect of true expansion can feel unsettling, as it challenges our comfort zone and familiar limits.

> *"A journey of a thousand miles begins with a single step."*
> —*Lao Tzu*

It's important to start in small, manageable steps. For example, someone dreaming of finding their future partner may feel disheartened if they expect an immediate, perfect connection. A grounded first step, however, might be to build self-love first, nurturing a deep relationship with oneself. This will help them approach future relationships from a place of inner wholeness, creating space for a healthier, more fulfilling partnership.

These gradual steps help us familiarise ourselves with our inner landscape, allowing us to notice when and where doubts or resistance surface. By stepping gradually with our personal rhythm and inner alignment, we come to understand how our unique manifestation journey unfolds.

Taking small steps also respects our nervous system, which can feel destabilised by sudden leaps into the unknown. Small, intentional steps allow us to expand at our own pace, helping to mitigate overwhelm and self-sabotage as we pursue our dreams. This is like building a muscle; it steadily builds strength (trust and confidence) without damage from excess pressure. We'll explore this further in the Mother archetype, which emphasises building stable foundations for sustainable growth.

Gaining Clarity of Vision

When we rely too heavily on others for direction, we risk falling into naivety and idealism. Naivety emerges when we accept others' guidance at face value, trusting that they know (and want) what's best for us without questioning if it aligns with our own desires. This lack of autonomy can lead to patterns of people-pleasing, where we overlook red flags or quiet our intuition to gain approval.

Idealism amplifies and is where we see the world through 'rose-tinted glasses' without conducting proper research, critical analysis, or considering the practical steps or challenges involved, resulting in frustration when reality doesn't match our expectations.

We can better navigate these obstacles with independent thinking to critically assess the advice and guidance of others while remaining clear in our vision. By developing greater autonomy, we learn to value our insights over external validation and pursue our dreams rooted in what truly resonates with us.

Commitment to a Clear Direction

The abundance of endless possibilities in the dreaming phase can lead to overwhelm and **indecisiveness.** Faced with too many choices, we may become scattered or paralysed.

This tendency can arise from a fear of making the 'wrong' choice, where opening the door to commit to one dream feels like missing other doors and opportunities. As a result, we jump between ideas, never fully nurturing any of them to fruition, or have many ideas or projects that never get finished, leading to a lack of direction and clarity.

The Maiden invites us to embrace the joy of possibility, teaching us the importance of narrowing our focus and committing to one path, trusting that new opportunities will emerge from this commitment.

Inspiration as the Antidote to Self-Doubt

Another obstacle related to the Maiden that many of us often experience is **imposter syndrome**—the fear that we're not truly capable or that we'll be 'found out' as 'frauds.' Despite clear evidence of our potential, this shadow of self-doubt can lead us to procrastinate, over-prepare, or avoid opportunities entirely. We may delay action, hesitating to step outside our comfort zone as we wait to feel 'ready' or 'worthy' to move forward. In these moments, the inner critic emerges, holding us back from realising our dreams.

The Maiden's energy of inspiration actively combats self-doubt by shifting our focus from fear to possibility. When we connect with inspiration, we are drawn toward our dreams, reducing the power of hesitation and the voice of the inner critic. This energy empowers us to recognise and quiet the voice of doubt as it fills us with enthusiasm and clarity of purpose.

The Maiden's journey teaches us that each inspired step forward lessens the grip of self-doubt, allowing our confidence to grow. Through inspiration, we learn that acting from a place of excitement and passion gradually dissolves self-doubt, revealing our true potential.

From Naivety to Clarity

> The betrayal in my job began when I was offered what seemed like a prestigious opportunity: a leadership role that aligned with my professional goals. My superiors assured me that the title of 'director' was merely a formality, requiring little from me beyond signing

a few documents occasionally, which they insisted would greatly help them out. Without much thought, I agreed, eager to please and trusting their reassurances.

It wasn't until two years later, when applying for a house loan, that I realised the implications. I was legally responsible for the company's actions as the Acting Director, a reality they had downplayed. This marked the moment I took off the rose-tinted glasses and saw the truth. I began to spiral as I realised how frequently they had gaslit me.

For example, I was quickly dismissed when I raised concerns about their irregular practice of charging clients in foreign currencies, which often resulted in unexpectedly higher fees. They brushed off my concerns, saying my clients were simply 'being difficult,' even questioning my understanding, asking, "Who are you to challenge the expertise of a top international law firm?"

Despite my instincts, I ignored my discomfort and continued trusting their assurances.

Even after deciding to leave, my commitment to integrity kept me focused on properly closing my accounts and ensuring everything was in order. However, the owner of the company revoked my access to the office and systems the day before I could complete the final delivery. Despite my completion of work being agreed upon with the partners, the owner had a history of being cold and retributive to people who left the company and seemed intent on avoiding paying me for the six months of work. When I pointed out the short-sightedness of this decision and its impact on the business, they issued a cease-and-desist order to silence me. Consulting lawyers made the harsh reality clear: as the Acting Director, I was legally accountable for the company's actions. It didn't matter what they did to me—technically—I was the company despite having no real power.

This reflects the shadow of the Maiden; with naivety and a people-pleasing nature, I had ignored my instincts and placed blind faith in authority to gain approval and validation. This shadow ultimately disempowered me and blocked me from making aligned decisions that served my highest good.

This painful lesson forced me to step back and reclaim the gift of clarity of vision. Reflecting on the experience, I realised I needed to trust myself and make decisions based on my values rather than seek external approval. This clarity provided me with a new slate where I could reimagine what I truly wanted for my career and life, pushing me to explore new possibilities.

The path was through curiosity. Instead of feeling stuck, I saw this as a chance to press 'reset' and ask, "Where is life going to take me next?" At first, I felt overwhelmed by the options and fearful of repeating past mistakes. But rather than focusing on details and trying to control the outcome, I let go of the 'how' and allowed myself time to dream about how I wanted to feel in my next role. By doing this, I embraced the gift of limitless dreaming and began approaching my career with a newfound openness and playfulness, trusting that life would guide me towards the right path.

Journal Prompts

1. What ignites a sense of wonder and playfulness in me?
   If nothing comes to mind, reflect on the last time you felt truly playful or imagine what moments might bring this energy into your life now.

2. What dreams did I hold as a child, and how do I feel about them now?
   Reflect on how your childhood dreams might reveal hidden desires and how you can weave that energy into your present life.

3. What limiting beliefs keep my dreams in the 'someday' category?
   Identify any beliefs that hold you back and explore how to take action despite them.

4. If I designed my dream life from scratch, without constraints, what would it look and feel like?
   Visualise every detail, focusing on what makes this vision fulfilling and unique to you.

5. Where in my life do I rely on external validation?
   Explore how the need for approval influences your decisions and what steps you can take to reclaim autonomy in pursuing your desires.

From Maiden to Lover

The Maiden has unlocked the limitless potential of dreaming. Now, with our vision set, the Lover takes the next step in the manifestation process—infusing those dreams with life force energy. This phase ensures that what once was only an idea now has the vitality to grow and materialise.

CHAPTER 2
The Lover Archetype: The Passionate Embodier

"Your visions will become clear only when you can look into your own heart. Who looks outside, dreams. Who looks inside, awakes."

—Carl Jung

THE LOVER EMBODIES manifestation emotionally and sensorially, transforming the Maiden's abstract dreams into vivid, felt experiences. Working in tandem with the Magician's envisioned pathways, the Lover grounds these possibilities in the present, creating a magnetic resonance that draws desires into being.

In this phase, emotions become powerful carriers of life force, infusing our desires with passion, joy, and love. By fully embodying our dreams as if they are already a reality, the Lover bridges the gap between where we are now and where we want to be, amplifying the manifestation process. This grounded presence lays the foundation for creation, enabling us to manifest a life rich in meaning and fulfilment.

Her energy is magnetic, naturally attracting people, opportunities, and experiences that are aligned with our intentions. This alignment between vision and embodiment accelerates manifestation, turning potential into reality and making manifestation a natural extension of who we are.

Chapter 2 – The Lover Archetype: The Passionate Embodier

When we resist the Lover's invitation to embody our desires, we lose connection with the emotional and sensory energies that fuel our dreams. This detachment weakens our attraction, leaving us uninspired and slowing the manifestation process. Without fully engaging her energy, we disrupt our foundation for creation and disconnect from the flow that brings our dreams to life.

The Inside Players: Master the Manifestation Game

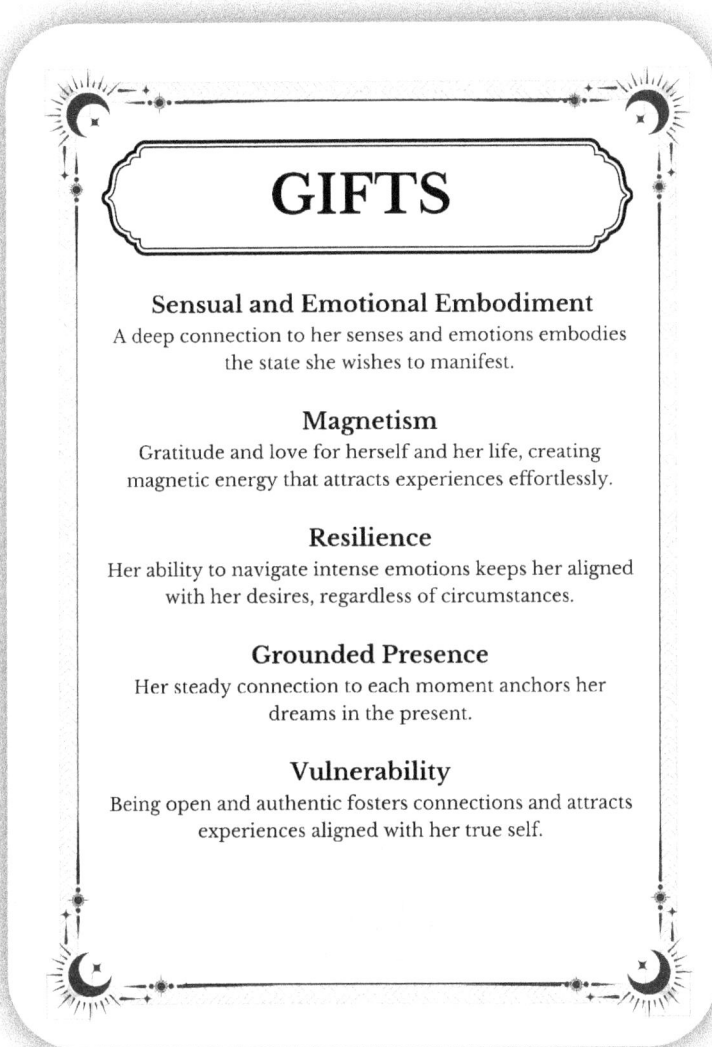

GIFTS

Sensual and Emotional Embodiment
A deep connection to her senses and emotions embodies the state she wishes to manifest.

Magnetism
Gratitude and love for herself and her life, creating magnetic energy that attracts experiences effortlessly.

Resilience
Her ability to navigate intense emotions keeps her aligned with her desires, regardless of circumstances.

Grounded Presence
Her steady connection to each moment anchors her dreams in the present.

Vulnerability
Being open and authentic fosters connections and attracts experiences aligned with her true self.

Passion stirs the soul, setting dreams alight.

Chapter 2 – The Lover Archetype: The Passionate Embodier

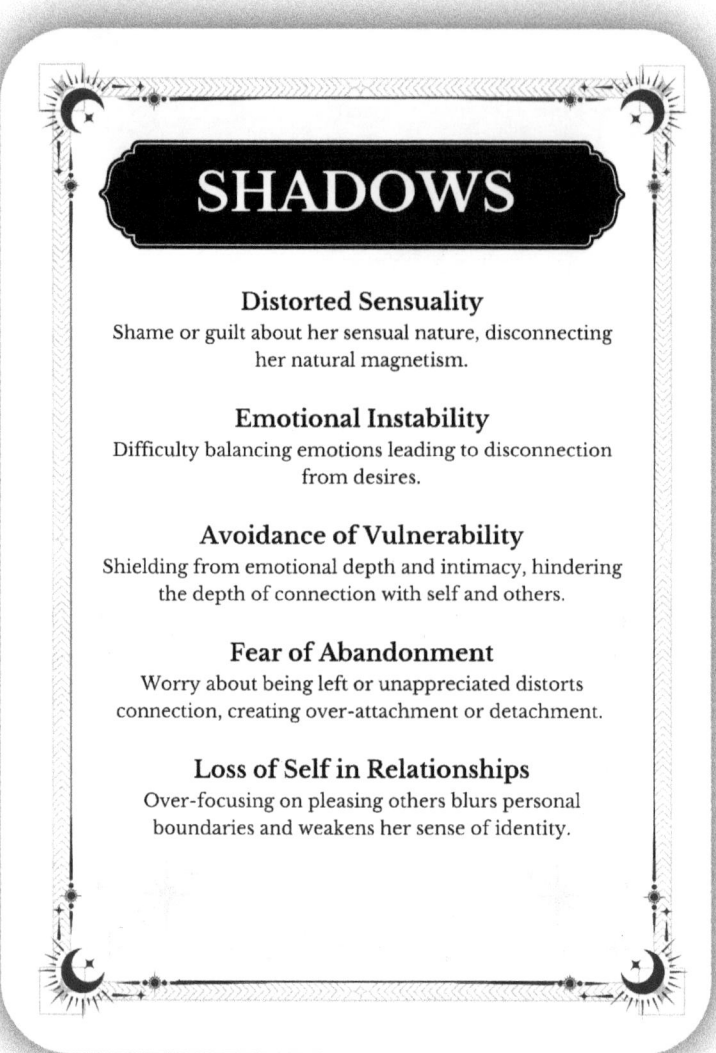

SHADOWS

Distorted Sensuality
Shame or guilt about her sensual nature, disconnecting her natural magnetism.

Emotional Instability
Difficulty balancing emotions leading to disconnection from desires.

Avoidance of Vulnerability
Shielding from emotional depth and intimacy, hindering the depth of connection with self and others.

Fear of Abandonment
Worry about being left or unappreciated distorts connection, creating over-attachment or detachment.

Loss of Self in Relationships
Over-focusing on pleasing others blurs personal boundaries and weakens her sense of identity.

To love without knowing oneself is to chase what cannot be found.

Overcoming the Obstacles of the Lover

The obstacles here arise when there is an imbalance in emotional energy or a shutting down of the Lover's vulnerability. The challenge is in learning to navigate emotional entanglements while maintaining an open heart without losing oneself.

Awakening Sensual Embodiment

Patriarchal conditioning has profoundly shaped how we relate to our bodies and emotions, often confusing sensuality with sexuality. This distorted sensuality fosters discomfort or shame around fully inhabiting our physical selves, leaving us feeling uneasy in our own bodies. Many of us also grew up in environments where emotions were criticised, invalidated, discouraged, or even completely disallowed.

Over time, this may result in becoming unable to be present within ourselves as a form of self-protection because any discomfort—whether physical or emotional—can feel inescapable. For the Lover, this discomfort can lead to **sensory over-indulgence**, where self-harm or sensory pleasures like alcohol, food, or beauty become ways to escape emotions rather than experience them fully.

As a result, it's common in our society to exist outside of body-awareness. This detachment keeps us from noticing signals from our bodies, such as tension or butterflies in the stomach, that reveal the deep connection between our emotions and our body's physical responses. By ignoring these signals, we lose touch with our inner landscape, limiting our ability to access the power of presence.

> Distancing ourselves from emotional depth puts us at risk of losing authentic self-connection. Vulnerability may feel overwhelming, leading us to shut down or experience emotional instability, insecurities, or a sense of not being loved.

Chapter 2 – The Lover Archetype: The Passionate Embodier

> We may even seek intensity or drama as a source of validation. Cultivating psychological and emotional safety helps us manage these emotions, build emotional resilience, and reconnect with ourselves.

These defences that may have once protected us eventually become barriers that limit deep connection and block the natural flow of abundance and fulfilment. In this closed-off state, we struggle to receive our desires, hindering manifestation. To dissolve these barriers, the Lover invites us to reclaim sensual embodiment, reconnect with our bodies, and welcome a deeper flow of presence, connection, and joy into our lives.

The Role of the Nervous System in Emotional Resilience

Emotional resilience is our ability to adapt, recover, and grow stronger through life's challenges, helping us to build character by cultivating inner strength. The Lover provides the resilience that enables us to process difficult emotions without becoming stuck in lower-vibrational states like fear or frustration, which create a sense of heaviness, disconnection, and a negative feedback loop.

Resilience requires emotional flexibility—the ability to welcome and experience a full range of emotions with tenderness and acceptance. By embracing and processing denser emotions, we create space for lighter, higher-vibrational states like love, joy, and gratitude. These states foster feelings of expansiveness, connection, and creativity, aligning us with the energy of manifestation.

When stress arises, resilience also allows us to recognise internal triggers, such as a racing heart or spiralling thoughts, and create a conscious pause. Mindfulness is a key tool here, helping us interrupt these repetitive reactive cycles, re-engage the rational mind, and shift into connection. These build the foundation for higher-vibrational living.

> **What is an Amygdala Hijack?**
>
> Stress activates the 'fight, flight or freeze' response of the sympathetic nervous system (SNS). In moments of heightened stress, the amygdala (the brain's threat detection centre) overrides the rational mind, triggering an **amygdala hijack**. This reaction floods the body with stress hormones like cortisol and adrenaline, narrowing our focus and heightening reactivity.
>
> While vital in moments of physical danger, this response is often unnecessarily triggered by emotional stressors, making it difficult to stay grounded or connected to higher-vibrational states like love, joy, or trust. Emotional flexibility and mindfulness create the space to notice early signs of stress, re-engage the rational mind, and shift from impulsive reactions to thoughtful responses.

How Emotional Resilience Helps Interrupt Reactive Cycles

The Lover archetype invites us to break reactive cycles by cultivating awareness of our internal landscape and developing tools to manage emotional stress. This is achieved through **titration**— the practice of processing emotions in small, manageable doses. By addressing intense emotions like grief, frustration, or anger incrementally, we prevent overwhelm and reduce the likelihood of triggering a full-blown amygdala hijack.

The key principles of emotional resilience include:

- **Disrupting Reactive Patterns:** Mindfulness helps us notice early signs of stress, creating a pause that interrupts reactive cycles and re-engages the rational mind.
- **Processing Emotions Incrementally:** Titration reduces emotional intensity, strengthens flexibility, and prevents overwhelm.

- **Building Emotional Reserves:** Resilience acts as an emotional 'bank account,' ensuring we have the inner resources to face challenges with calm and confidence.

The Lover archetype reminds us that resilience is not about suppressing emotions but embracing them with tenderness and grace. Emotional flexibility helps us shift from lower-vibrational states like fear and frustration to higher-vibrational states like love and joy, anchoring us in connection and abundance. By cultivating resilience, the Lover transforms stress into an opportunity for alignment, helping us live with presence, balance, and the emotional depth essential for surrendered manifestation.

Building Magnetism Through Gratitude

The Lover also teaches us to build resilience and flexibility through **emotional shifting**—consciously moving from lower-vibrational emotions like fear or frustration to higher-vibrational states like love, joy, and gratitude.

> *"The brain cannot hold two opposing emotional states at once. Focusing on gratitude, love, or abundance naturally helps to override feelings of scarcity and fear."*

Gratitude plays a large role in this shift. When we focus on what we already have, we cultivate a sense of fullness and appreciation that naturally counteracts feelings of scarcity. This sense of fullness strengthens the Lover's personal magnetism, helping to counter insecurities that might otherwise lead us to rely on external affirmation or comparison. By embracing gratitude, we strengthen our connection to our self-worth and enhance our natural allure.

This state of gratitude also activates the parasympathetic nervous system (PNS; essentially the 'opposite' of the SNS), promoting calm and receptivity. Gratitude also rewires our neural pathways, making it easier to maintain a mindset of abundance and possibility. In addition, it boosts dopamine and serotonin, neurotransmitters that regulate happiness and emotional balance, further enhancing resilience and aligning us with the energy needed for manifestation.

The Positive Feedback Loop

The Lover's magnetism creates a positive feedback loop in which high-vibrational emotions attract experiences that reinforce them. The more we sustain these emotions, the more situations we attract that amplify them, creating a self-perpetuating cycle of abundance. For example, maintaining gratitude often invites kindness and positive changes in relationships, fostering an environment where people are more likely to support one another.

Taken to extremes, this feedback loop can lead to over-idealising situations, particularly in love and romance, where people or relationships are placed on a pedestal. This unconscious bias (explored further in Chapter 4 on the Huntress Archetype) may cause us to overlook red flags or misinterpret situations to maintain an idealised image. When reality inevitably falls short, our emotional balance is disrupted, leading to disillusionment, disappointment, or resentment.

To sustain a balanced positive feedback loop, it's essential to direct emotional energy mindfully, focusing on realistic and meaningful connections. Practising gratitude, love, and joy aligns us with abundance, but true harmony comes from embracing the full spectrum of life—the highs and lows alike. By honouring both with awareness, we ground ourselves in presence, attune more deeply to the energy we emit, and empower ourselves to respond consciously rather than impulsively.

From Emotional Instability to Vulnerability

For many years, I struggled with periodic depression, relying on emotional highs to get through the day. Like a sugar crash, these highs would eventually give way to deep lows that left me unable to get out of bed. This constant search for emotional highs was a way to avoid deeper pain, but only offered temporary relief, never addressing the underlying issues. This cycle was a manifestation of the Lover's shadow of emotional instability and avoidance. Stress often overwhelmed me, and I turned to alcohol and occasional drug use to numb the pain.

One night, after drinking too much, I had a major argument with my boyfriend (now husband). The next day, still raw from the argument, I overdosed on MDMA at a festival. My body reacted violently, and after hours of vomiting, my throat swelled so badly from the acid that it nearly closed. I spent the night sucking on ice cubes to reduce the swelling.

I didn't know how to deal with my suffering, so I compartmentalised everything and distanced myself from vulnerability. I was raised in a household shaped by Chinese cultural values, where *saving face* was paramount, and I was taught that sharing personal struggles was a sign of embarrassment and shame. Once, for example, when I confided in a cousin about my mum's abusive boyfriend, the word got back to her. Her anger and sense of betrayal left me feeling deeply ashamed for speaking out. From that moment, I buried my emotions, believing vulnerability was both unsafe and isolating.

Of course, these boxed emotions didn't just vanish; they became embedded in my body, creating emotional resistance that made it harder to maintain any real balance. I avoided vulnerability and swung between emotional highs and deep lows, unable to sustain a healthy emotional rhythm. I used my independence as a shield, keeping others at arm's length to avoid getting hurt. For about a year, my thoughts darkened to the point where I considered death every day. My partner tried to encourage me to think positively, but no amount of positivity could lift the weight I was carrying. I wanted to escape the misery in my body because it felt unbearable.

One day, he opened up to me about how challenging it was for him to carry the weight of my depression. His willingness to be vulnerable and express his own struggle created a moment of deep connection that shifted the shame within me. I realised I wasn't alone in this journey and that true connection required me to release the barriers I had built around myself. This realisation encouraged me to begin working on internal resistance. As I released this dense emotion, staying present in my body became less of a struggle, and I began cultivating a sense of safety and openness within myself.

Over time, it became easier to sustain the balance of higher vibrational states like gratitude and joy. What once felt like fleeting moments of alignment became my new normal, which built an emotional reservoir to navigate adversity. In reclaiming the Lover's gifts of emotional depth, authentic connection, and presence, I transformed how I experienced life.

My heart opened, allowing me to embrace life's highs and lows as essential parts of my journey. Instead of resisting the painful moments in life, each experience taught me resilience, deepening my capacity for authentic connection.

Journal Prompts

1. When I envision my biggest dreams, how do they feel in my body?
   Notice if your body responds with excitement, tension, or calm.

2. How would it feel to live as though my dreams have already manifested?
   Imagine yourself living as if your desires were already fulfilled. Notice how your posture, energy, and interactions transform with this embodiment.

3. What are three things I'm grateful for right now, and how can I express gratitude for them?
   Focus on turning gratitude into real and tangible expressions of appreciation.

4. Where in my life could I embrace vulnerability more fully?
   Reflect on areas where openness could deepen your connections and help you feel more authentically seen, perhaps by recalling a situation where you felt unseen.

5. What is my relationship with self-love, and how does it influence my daily life?
   Reflect on how you nurture or neglect self-love, and consider its impact on your actions, choices, and emotional well-being.

From Lover to Mother

The Lover breathes life into our dreams through sensory and emotional embodiment, infusing them with vibrancy. Her role is to charge the dream with passion, making it feel real and in the present. In contrast, the Mother's role is to create a sacred, safe space where dreams can grow. By supporting the container for growth, the Mother ensures that what has been inspired by the Lover can take root and flourish.

CHAPTER 3
The Mother Archetype: The Sacred Container

"Be like a tree and let the dead leaves drop."

—*Rumi*

THE MOTHER IS the nurturing container of manifestation, where the seeds planted by the Maiden and infused with life by the Lover are held and grounded to take root.

This phase requires us to shift from envisioning and embodying to creating stability and space for our visions to grow. Receptivity is essential in surrendered manifestation, but we can only receive as much as we are able to hold. 'Holding' involves creating a stable and nurturing container that provides the space, support, and protection needed for our dreams to mature.

Like a tree shedding its leaves to make way for new growth, the Mother's energy is one of renewal and expansion. This natural cycle creates space within, aligning us with what truly supports our intentions. By balancing growth with containment, the Mother cultivates a spacious, supportive environment. This includes regulating our nervous system, which increases our capacity to receive and ensures our manifestations are sustainable and aligned with our purpose.

When we neglect the Mother's wisdom, our inner space can feel restricted or unstable, making it difficult for our dreams to thrive—like a plant with shallow roots. Without the Mother's support, we risk receiving desires without the structure to hold them. Honouring the Mother creates a balanced environment where our manifestations can flourish, supported by stability and aligned with our capacity for growth.

The Inside Players: Master the Manifestation Game

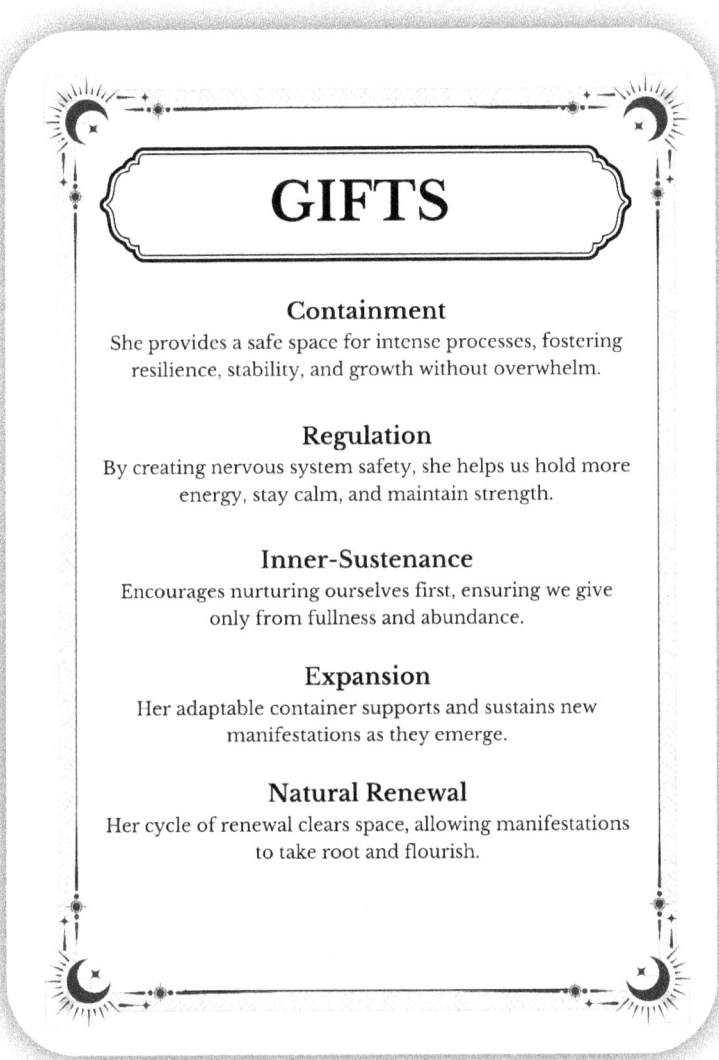

GIFTS

Containment
She provides a safe space for intense processes, fostering resilience, stability, and growth without overwhelm.

Regulation
By creating nervous system safety, she helps us hold more energy, stay calm, and maintain strength.

Inner-Sustenance
Encourages nurturing ourselves first, ensuring we give only from fullness and abundance.

Expansion
Her adaptable container supports and sustains new manifestations as they emerge.

Natural Renewal
Her cycle of renewal clears space, allowing manifestations to take root and flourish.

What is tended with care will bloom in its own time.

Chapter 3 – The Mother Archetype: The Sacred Container

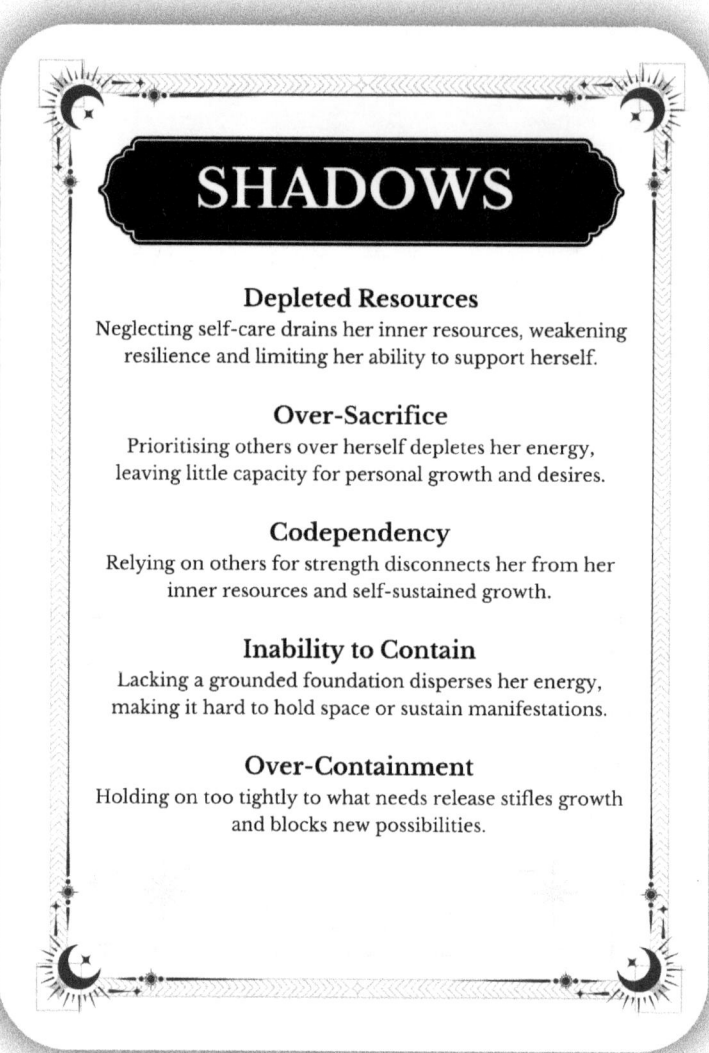

SHADOWS

Depleted Resources
Neglecting self-care drains her inner resources, weakening resilience and limiting her ability to support herself.

Over-Sacrifice
Prioritising others over herself depletes her energy, leaving little capacity for personal growth and desires.

Codependency
Relying on others for strength disconnects her from her inner resources and self-sustained growth.

Inability to Contain
Lacking a grounded foundation disperses her energy, making it hard to hold space or sustain manifestations.

Over-Containment
Holding on too tightly to what needs release stifles growth and blocks new possibilities.

A field left untended grows wild, but a field never emptied cannot be sown.

> Inner resources are the personal reserves we draw upon to support ourselves physically, mentally, and emotionally. They include physical vitality, mental clarity, emotional resilience, and self-regulation skills. Strengthening these helps us sustain growth, remain grounded, and expands our capacity to hold what we manifest.

Overcoming the Obstacles of the Mother

The Mother's obstacles stem from over-nurturing or holding on to outdated energies. Failing to release what no longer serves her can congest her container of growth, blocking the flow of new manifestations. Her challenge is continually refreshing her energy to allow new possibilities to flourish.

Building a Sustainable Container

As we stretch our limits to break through personal ceilings and expand into new ways of being, we will inevitably encounter experiences that overstimulate our nervous system. In these moments, heightened physiological responses—such as increased cortisol—can disrupt our equilibrium, making it challenging to stay grounded and open to manifestation. This is when the nervous system's ability to return to balance becomes crucial; otherwise, we risk being unable to contain our dreams.

The **Polyvagal Theory** explains how the function of the vagus nerve transitions us from the fight or flight response governed by the SNS to the calm, restorative state of the PNS. However, it's important to note that the freeze response does not exclusively belong to either system. Instead, it can arise from an interplay between extreme states of sympathetic arousal (overactivation) and dorsal vagal shutdown (a collapse of energy), creating immobilisation as a protective mechanism.

Building on the emotional resilience cultivated by the Lover archetype, the Mother helps us deepen nervous system regulation by grounding intense responses and shifting us from survival mode into a receptive, balanced state. This transition expands our **Window of Tolerance**—the range within which we can process emotions and navigate challenges without becoming overwhelmed.

The Mother archetype introduces the concept of containment, the ability to hold and stabilise emotional energy without needing to release it immediately. Containment allows us to remain present and aligned, even in moments of heightened emotional or energetic intensity. It can take many forms:

- **Setting boundaries** to protect our energy and prevent emotional overextension.
- **Compartmentalising emotions**, consciously setting them aside to process later when we feel more capable.
- **Using grounding practices**, such as breathwork, sensory awareness, or visualisations, to stabilise intense responses in the moment.
- **Creating physical containers**, like writing down emotions in a journal and setting them aside.
- **Movement-based containment**, such as walking or slow stretching to channel emotional energy safely.

By combining these practices with titration, we learn to release energy gradually while strengthening our capacity to hold space for intensity. This ensures we prevent emotional overwhelm or collapse, allowing us to expand into new ways of being.

> *"Just as we wouldn't open a shaken soda bottle all at once, the Mother's container allows us to release and process intense emotions in a controlled, balanced way, preventing an overwhelming surge of energy that triggers a stress response."*

By cultivating this grounded stability, the Mother expands our capacity for emotional resilience and integration, supporting us in sustaining and nurturing our manifestations without destabilising our system.

Building Inner Resources

As humans, our emotional well-being is supported by internal and external resources. **Co-regulation**, where people help each other manage emotions, is a natural and vital part of our emotional ecosystem. It fosters connection and provides relief in times of stress. However, the Mother archetype reminds us that over-reliance on external support can hinder personal growth and emotional independence.

When we depend too heavily on others for reassurance or solutions, we risk creating a cycle of enmeshment, where emotional stability becomes overly tied to external sources. For instance, someone who frequently relies on turning to friends or family for support during challenges, seeking validation or guidance to navigate difficult emotions. While this can provide temporary relief, it often limits personal growth by preventing us from developing our own inner resources.

On a deeper level, this reliance reflects a surrender of personal power. It signals to the universe that we are not yet ready to fully receive our manifestations.

The Mother archetype helps us overcome this obstacle by teaching us to cultivate our own inner resources through the development of self-regulation. Self-regulation provides the stability needed to navigate life's challenges with confidence, strengthening our ability to hold space for manifestations and aligning us with the energy of self-sufficiency.

This foundational practice forms the basis of personal power, which extends outward through the King archetype, where it matures into external authority and leadership.

Navigating Expansion with Ease

Growth and expansion can be uncomfortable, like training for a marathon. This is natural as we move beyond what we thought possible. However, not all discomfort is equal. The distorted masculine approach to manifestation often misinterprets discomfort as 'hustle'—the belief that if you're not struggling, you're not progressing. But misaligned hustle traps us in resistance, drains our energy, and disconnects us from our true purpose.

For example, consider a career shift. When we are aligned, learning new skills or adapting to responsibilities feels energising and fulfilling. But when discomfort becomes draining, like pushing against a wall, it signals misalignment or overexertion.

True growth stretches your limits but should feel expansive and sustainable, not depleting. This is where the Mother's wisdom is essential. Her nurturing energy counters the distorted masculine mindset, teaching us to approach discomfort with grace and balance. She also creates space for renewal—whether it's time to reflect, energy to reset, or emotional bandwidth to process—allowing growth to feel supportive rather than overwhelming.

When growth feels like a constant uphill battle, the Mother reminds us to release what no longer serves us. In doing so, she transforms discomfort into aligned growth that expands our capacity while keeping us grounded and regulated.

Expanding at the Right Pace

While expansion brings natural discomfort, a key challenge in the Mother phase is resisting the urge to expand too quickly. Rapid growth may seem appealing, but by forcing expansion before our emotional container is ready, we are on a path to instability and burnout. This 'inability to contain' can overwhelm the nervous system, leading to anxiety, exhaustion, emotional overload, or amygdala hijack. To prevent burnout and maintain stability, we must titrate our progress in manageable doses.

> *"Much like a plant requires time to grow into a larger pot, our inner capacity must evolve gradually to hold the energy of new manifestations."*

The Mother archetype reminds us that true growth unfolds in its divine timing. Just as we can't rush a child's development, we can't hasten the expansion of our inner capacity. Trusting in the natural flow of growth ensures we develop long-term resilience and balance, creating a stable environment where our desires can flourish without overwhelming our system.

Of course, sometimes manifestations happen quickly, and we will explore this more in Chapter 9 on the Magician archetype. However, the Mother's role is to ensure that growth is sustainable.

Nurturing Inner Sustenance

Another common obstacle in the Mother phase is the tendency to 'over-sacrifice' or fall into a **martyrdom** mindset. While nurturing and supporting others is a natural expression of the Mother archetype, giving from a place of depletion rather than abundance weakens our energetic container and limits our ability to receive.

Constantly prioritising the needs of others at the expense of our own creates an imbalance, leaving us drained and unable to sustain our manifestations. Giving beyond our capacity also signals that we're not yet able to hold greater abundance in our lives.

The Mother archetype reminds us that boundaries are an essential form of self-care necessary for sustainable giving. By prioritising our needs and respecting our energetic limits, we create the space to replenish and expand our capacity for giving and receiving. By honouring our well-being, we create a self-renewing foundation that supports the flow of abundance into our lives, allowing us to give freely and from a place of fulfilment.

From Over-Containment to Increased Capacity

Before embracing vulnerability, my coping mechanisms reflected the Mother shadow of over-containment. I boxed my emotions, numbed myself, and compartmentalised everything in an attempt to maintain control. I believed that keeping everything tightly held would help me manage. Instead, it disconnected me from my emotions and stopped me from addressing what truly needed attention. Over time, my nervous system became overloaded with unresolved stress, preventing me from manifesting the peace and success I longed for.

I turned to alcohol to avoid confronting difficult feelings, which created emotional distance in my relationships and made healthy co-regulation with others nearly impossible. Storing stress in my body left me constantly on edge, unable to process or release my emotions. This cycle of over-containment kept me stuck and unable to move forward.

Two key shifts helped me transform: firstly, I released emotions that no longer served me, creating space for growth. Secondly, I learned to self-regulate during difficulties without relying on unhealthy habits. This created a stable foundation for growth as it allowed me to manage greater levels of stress while staying grounded and connected. With a more regulated nervous system, I began to handle challenges in ways that felt expansive rather than overwhelming.

The Mother nurtures growth by teaching us to expand our emotional capacity gradually. For example, when I became pregnant, I was overwhelmed by the available advice about the inevitable loss of sleep, personal time, and freedom that comes with parenthood. The sheer volume of opinions felt suffocating. However, instead of spiralling into anxiety, I chose to embody the self-nurturing qualities of the Mother, shutting out the noise and creating space to process these changes at *my own pace*. By prioritising self-care, I gained the stability needed to approach these transitions in a titrated and sustainable way.

After my son was born, I eventually returned to work. I reintegrated gradually, starting with just a few hours a day before building up to full-time work (on top of motherhood and studying for my trauma-informed Sacred Leadership certificate!). This gradual reintegration (another example of titration) allowed me to expand my capacity without overwhelm, focusing on what needed greater attention.

Through the cycle of renewal and releasing outdated processes, I built the capacity to grow without overwhelm. This shift allowed me to meet life's demands while expanding my ability to hold greater abundance aligned with my deepest self.

Journal Prompts

1. In what areas am I ready to stretch and expand?
   Map out where you feel ready to grow physically, emotionally, and energetically, and envision what this new level of expansion could look like for you.

2. What inspires me to keep expanding, even when it's challenging?
   Identify what motivates you to continue growing despite discomfort or obstacles. Consider how this inspiration can serve as a steadying force when you encounter resistance.

3. What signals tell me I'm entering a growth period?
   Notice how your body and emotions respond to periods of change and expansion, and describe any patterns you notice in how you approach growth.

4. How do I regulate my emotions when I encounter challenges?

Reflect on your typical responses to adversity and consider which tools or practices help you stay grounded and resilient.

5. Do I show up for myself in the same way that I show up for others?
    Reflect on how you can nurture yourself emotionally, mentally, and physically.

From Mother to Huntress

As we have seen, the Mother nurtures and strengthens the container of manifestation, ensuring it can sustain the growth of our dreams over time. By staying attuned to our inner world and building our inner reserves, she provides a stable foundation for abundance. Once this container is fortified, the Huntress takes the lead, fearlessly clearing outdated beliefs and resistance. Her courage and precision ensure that the path to manifestation is clear and aligned, allowing us to boldly move ahead.

CHAPTER 4
The Huntress Archetype: The Truth Seeker

"The obstacle is the path."

—*Zen Proverb*

The Huntress marks the shift from setting up the container to clearing it, inviting us to confront and remove unseen barriers that hinder our dreams.

In this phase of manifestation, the Huntress gives us the courage to seek out and address the edges of our resistance. She encourages us to become accountable and delve into the hidden parts of our psyche, uncovering fears, limiting beliefs, and patterns that no longer serve us. Through this inner work, she ensures our path is free of resistance and aligned with our vision so our dreams can unfold without interference.

Her energy embodies the fierce determination and resolve of a spiritual warrior. She empowers us to uncover and confront the subconscious patterns misaligned with our conscious intentions, paving the way to restore our full power of manifestation.

When we fail to engage with the Huntress, we risk remaining unaware of the hidden forces sabotaging our efforts. Without her courage, we stay trapped in cycles of frustration and self-sabotage, questioning why our progress stalls. By stepping into her energy, we gain clarity and the freedom to move forward without resistance.

Chapter 4 – The Huntress Archetype: The Truth Seeker

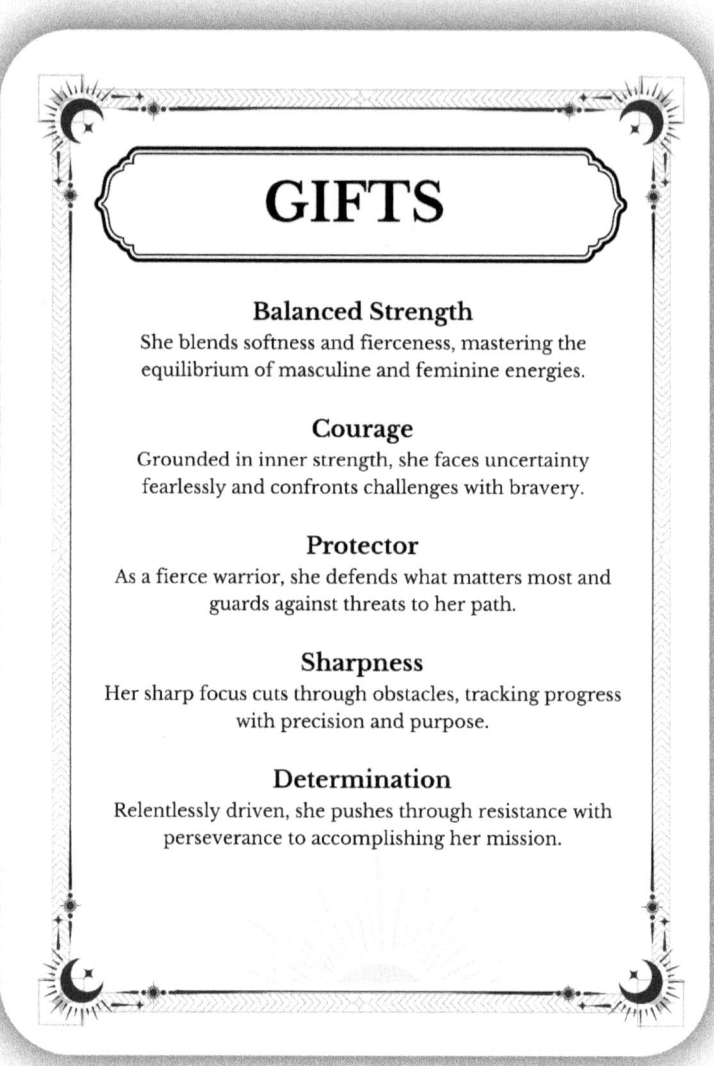

GIFTS

Balanced Strength
She blends softness and fierceness, mastering the equilibrium of masculine and feminine energies.

Courage
Grounded in inner strength, she faces uncertainty fearlessly and confronts challenges with bravery.

Protector
As a fierce warrior, she defends what matters most and guards against threats to her path.

Sharpness
Her sharp focus cuts through obstacles, tracking progress with precision and purpose.

Determination
Relentlessly driven, she pushes through resistance with perseverance to accomplishing her mission.

She who knows her target wastes no arrows.

The Inside Players: Master the Manifestation Game

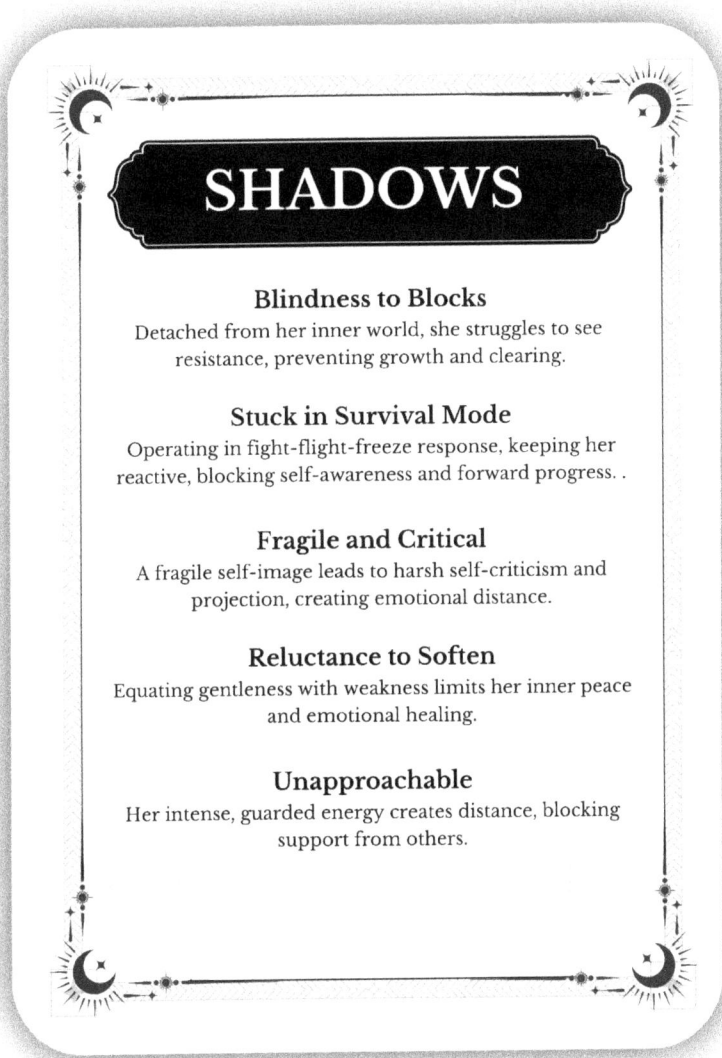

SHADOWS

Blindness to Blocks
Detached from her inner world, she struggles to see resistance, preventing growth and clearing.

Stuck in Survival Mode
Operating in fight-flight-freeze response, keeping her reactive, blocking self-awareness and forward progress. .

Fragile and Critical
A fragile self-image leads to harsh self-criticism and projection, creating emotional distance.

Reluctance to Soften
Equating gentleness with weakness limits her inner peace and emotional healing.

Unapproachable
Her intense, guarded energy creates distance, blocking support from others.

A hunter lost in doubt will mistake their own reflection for prey.

Overcoming the Obstacles of the Huntress

The Huntress archetype represents the courage to face the hidden fears and subconscious resistance that hinder manifestation. These obstacles, such as self-doubt, limiting beliefs, or unresolved patterns, keep us stuck in misalignment. The Huntress seeks to uncover these barriers, clearing the way for aligned action and growth.

Determination to Hunt Resistance

Subconscious resistance often manifests as recurring patterns, unexplained challenges, or missed opportunities that trap us in an endless loop. The Huntress sees these obstacles as purposeful signals to explore deeper layers of the psyche. With fierce focus and accountability, she uncovers the limitations and protective mechanisms that hold her back. By identifying and transforming the roots of resistance, she creates the space needed for new possibilities to emerge.

> *"We are all blind to what we don't foresee."*
> —John Locke

As Carl Jung's theory of individuation suggests, the path to wholeness requires integrating the fragmented aspects of ourselves—those shaped by past experiences, inherited beliefs, and societal conditioning. The Huntress views these resistances as opportunities to reclaim hidden pieces of herself. By recognising their protective role and confronting their roots, she transforms these resistances into stepping stones, paving the way for the Healer to rewire her inner world to align with the future self she is seeking to become.

The Obstacles Behind Manifestation Blocks

As discussed in the Introduction, there are three main categories of manifestation blocks: expansion, alignment, and abundance blocks (see page 10). These blocks are signalled by the obstacles we experience, often shaped by deeper layers of our subconscious patterns and rooted in the shadows of our psyche. The Huntress is uniquely equipped to uncover these hidden layers, identifying the psychological, spiritual, and energetic roots of resistance. By addressing these origins, she reveals how shadows create patterns that limit us, offering a pathway to reclaim power and align with our manifestation potential.

These take the form of the following obstacles that the Huntress must overcome:

- **Scarcity Mindset:** A fear of lack that limits our ability to see or attract abundance.
- **Inner Child Wounds:** Unresolved experiences tied to self-worth, love, or safety that hinder our ability to receive.
- **Energetic Imbalance:** Emotional or physical tension from past trauma, stress, or unresolved emotions that disrupts energy flow and hinders alignment.
- **The Inner Critic:** Self-doubt and negative inner talk that lead to self-sabotage.
- **Ancestral Patterns:** Limiting beliefs passed down through generations.
- **Collective Conditioning:** Cultural norms and societal pressures that reinforce restrictive beliefs.

Our personal trauma history plays a big part in shaping our experiences and influencing how we engage with the world, including creating deep resistance. However, these sources of resistance also stem from parts of us that hold on to limitations as a form of protection.

For example, the need for perfection might have once helped us gain approval or avoid criticism. However, it prevents us from taking meaningful action later in life, leaving us stuck in a cycle of overthinking and self-doubt.

> *"The Huntress, the spiritual warrior, helps us to understand our subconscious patterns, empowering us to acknowledge, thank, and release them."*

Chapter 4 – The Huntress Archetype: The Truth Seeker

The Huntress embodies the fierce determination to identify and dismantle the patterns and resistance created by shadows that stifle our expansion, alignment, and abundance.

Sharpness to Identify Internalised Defences

One of the most challenging obstacles the Huntress faces is to break through internalised defence mechanisms. These are unconscious psychological strategies that have been absorbed or adopted, often from early caregivers or social environments, to shield oneself from emotional distress, anxiety, or perceived threats. These subconscious patterns often arise when the SNS 'survival mode' is activated, offering a sense of safety by shielding us from discomfort. However, as every protective wall can also become a prison wall, it can trap us in cycles of resistance, creating defensiveness that impairs the clarity needed to learn, grow, and align.

Internalised defences obscure awareness and mask deeply held beliefs and behaviours that perpetuate resistance. Common examples include:

- **Internalised Marginalisation**: Absorbing beliefs from cultural or societal conditioning that limit one's sense of potential and self-worth. For instance, a woman raised to believe that leadership is 'for men' may doubt her capabilities in a leadership role.
- **Idealisation of the Oppressor**: Unconscious admiration of those in power, often to gain acceptance or self-worth. For example, an employee may idealise a harsh boss, seeing their behaviour as 'strong leadership' and emulating it, even at personal cost.
- **Cognitive Dissonance Reduction**: Adjusting beliefs or attitudes to reduce discomfort when the action doesn't align with a personal value. For instance, someone who values honesty may repeatedly stay silent about their needs in a relationship to avoid conflict.
- **Trauma Bond**: Emotional attachment formed through cycles of love and mistreatment, making it hard to leave harmful situations. For example, someone may stay in a toxic relationship,

feeling compelled to endure the mistreatment due to fleeting moments of affection.
- **Projecting Insecurity**: Attributing personal insecurities or fears to others to avoid facing them. For example, someone who feels inadequate at work might assume their colleagues think they're unqualified, deflecting self-doubt rather than addressing it.

By hunting for these moments of internal tension, the Huntress helps us bring awareness of when we are out of alignment. She empowers us to confront the discomfort, dismantle these defences, and realign with our values.

Table 2 Examples of unconscious bias.

Unconscious Bias	Description
Affinity	Preferring people who are similar to us in some way, such as background or interests.
Confirmation	Seeking out information that confirms our pre-existing beliefs or assumptions, often overlooking contradictory evidence.
Halo Effect	Viewing one positive quality in a person (like attractiveness or intelligence) as a sign of overall positive traits.
Stereotyping	Making generalised assumptions about a person based on group characteristics, such as gender, race, or age.

These are just a few examples of types of unconscious bias, illustrating how ingrained assumptions can distort our perception of challenges. These defences distort our perception of challenges, making it harder to identify the true sources of resistance. They blind us to red flags, trapping us in recurring patterns that feel inexplicable and leaving us stuck beneath an invisible ceiling.

Breaking Through Defences

Fragility often arises when working with internalised defences, a challenge the Huntress instinctively recognises as she sharpens her focus on the roots of resistance. This triggers a protective mechanism, where she may retreat from situations that expose vulnerabilities, reinforcing a cycle of avoidance that feels safe but ultimately prevents meaningful growth.

This withdrawal deepens patterns of self-criticism, keeping the Huntress focused on perceived flaws and preventing us from recognising opportunities for change. Attempting to protect our insecurities can result in judging others, creating emotional distance, and isolating ourselves from supportive connections. Over time, this guardedness projects 'unapproachable' energy, making it difficult for others to create meaningful connections, perpetuating a deeper and deeper sense of isolation.

We awaken to deeper truths when the Huntress sharpens our focus and guides us to the roots of resistance. This act of accountability dismantles defences, unlocking clarity and alignment. By integrating shadows and embracing the wisdom this provides us, we reclaim our hidden potential and step fully into our innate power as creators of our reality.

Chakras and Manifestation

The cause of manifestation blocks can also be tracked as imbalances within the chakra system, an understanding of life energy (*prana*) flow through energy centres in the body (*chakra*) developed in India over millennia. Each chakra governs a specific area of life and energy flow. Manifestation begins at the **crown chakra**, where inspiration is born. It flows downward through each chakra, gaining momentum until it manifests in the physical world at the root chakra.

Table 3 shows the role chakra imbalances play in manifestation.

Table 3 Chakra imbalances and manifestation.

Chakra (descending order)	Role in Manifestation	Overactive	Underactive
Crown	Represents a connection to higher consciousness and divine inspiration. Imbalances obstruct the flow of ideas.	Overthinking, disconnected from the physical body.	Lack of inspiration, disconnection from spirit.
Third Eye	Governs intuition, vision, and imagination. Imbalances impair the clarity of purpose and visualisation.	Over-imaginative, seeing illusions.	Lack of clarity, difficulty envisioning the future.
Throat	Related to expression and communication. Imbalances limit our ability to speak our desires and express our truth.	Over-communicative dominating conversations.	Fear of speaking, inability to express oneself.
Heart	Tied to love, compassion, and relationships. Imbalances restrict us from aligning with the frequency of love.	Overly dependent in relationships.	Difficulty trusting, emotional isolation.
Solar Plexus	Governs personal power, confidence, and willpower. Imbalance distorts action, leading to domination or insecurity.	Controlling, overly competitive.	Low self-esteem, lack of personal power.
Sacral	Controls creativity and emotions. Imbalances disrupt the creative flow necessary for birthing new ideas.	Overly emotional, impulsive.	Difficulty in intimate relationships, stifling creativity.
Root	Represents security and grounding. Imbalances undermine stability and the ability to manifest in the material world.	Overly materialistic, fear-driven.	Lack of groundedness, insecurity.

Chapter 4 – The Huntress Archetype: The Truth Seeker

Energy flow is disrupted when a chakra is overactive or underactive. For instance, an imbalanced crown chakra might leave someone overwhelmed with ideas but unable to ground any of them in reality, as seen in the Maiden's tendency to remain stuck in 'dreamland.' These energetic imbalances prevent alignment, interrupting the natural flow needed to manifest desires.

Resolving these imbalances restores balance so energy can flow freely through the chakras to ground manifestations fully into reality.

From Blindness to Activating the Spiritual Warrior

There was a period when I felt like I'd hit a glass ceiling with my finances. No matter how hard I worked or tried, I couldn't seem to break through. Frustrated, I turned to meditation to explore what was holding me back.

One day, during an inner work session, I noticed a familiar sensation, a fluttering in my stomach that I'd felt countless times before. It was irritating, always lingering in the background but never fully addressed. This time, instead of brushing it off, I made the choice to sit with it, holding space for the feeling and simply observing.

As I stayed with the sensation, it began to shift. What had initially felt light and restless deepened into a tightening, like something being wrung out. It wasn't comfortable, but instead of pulling away, I leaned in, letting it guide me. Suddenly, a memory from my childhood surfaced.

I was at home during one of my parents' many arguments. My dad had recently returned from an offshore contract, and tensions were high amid accusations of infidelity. After months of explosive fights, my parents decided to reconcile, agreeing to work on their marriage and renovate the house as a symbol of a fresh start.

My mum confided in me that she feared the money would be spent elsewhere (namely, on mistresses), so she anchored it to debt, trying to protect it. Despite their efforts, the underlying issues in their relationship were never resolved, and money became a constant point of contention in our home.

From these experiences, as a child, I absorbed the belief that money wasn't 'safe' and it wasn't supportive; it was a weapon used to control and cause pain. Unconsciously, I carried this belief into adulthood. No matter how hard I worked, a part of me just didn't trust money. I saw it as dangerous—something that could be taken away or used against me. This subconscious belief had shaped my relationship with abundance, quietly sabotaging my efforts and keeping me stuck.

It wasn't until I shifted inward and tracked the energetic tension that I uncovered the source of resistance: my inner child's belief. Sitting with the discomfort of my physical symptoms, instead of pushing it away, allowed my body and mind to reveal the deeper truth. I connected with the inner child who had carried this belief for so long, reassuring her that the circumstances of the past no longer defined my life.

This act of reconciliation unlocked something profound within me. Within eight weeks, my income more than doubled. I witnessed firsthand the transformative power of manifesting from within. This experience awakened my spiritual warrior, giving me the determination to turn shadows into gifts and harness the power of surrendered manifestation. By releasing control and aligning with my inner truth, I unlocked a flow of abundance and purpose that continues to shape my life.

Chapter 4 – The Huntress Archetype: The Truth Seeker

Journal Prompts

1. What inner attitudes or beliefs shape how I explore my own limitations?
   Consider, for example, whether you approach inner work with curiosity, resistance, or judgement.

2. Do these limitations feel inherited from family, culture, or society?
   Examine if these patterns are rooted in family stories, cultural beliefs, or societal conditioning and how they've shaped your beliefs around success or worthiness.

3. What recurring patterns of limitation keep showing up in my life?
   Explore whether these limitations appear in relationships, careers, or self-worth. Consider how long they've been present and the cost of holding on to them.

4. Which archetypes resonate most with my current challenges or resistance?
   Reflect on which archetypes embody qualities you recognise in yourself.

5. What would my life look like if this resistance no longer existed?
   Consider what new opportunities might appear if this resistance was resolved.

From Huntress to Healer

After the Huntress uncovers the hidden players of resistance and clears the way, the Healer steps in to transmute those distortions from shadows into gifts. She anchors the path to align with the change we seek, ensuring the transformation is deeply rooted and lasting.

CHAPTER 5
The Healer Archetype: The Inner Transformer

"The flower that blooms in adversity is the most rare and beautiful of all."

—Walt Disney

The Healer is the revitalising force of manifestation, transforming past wounds and limitations into sources of inner strength.

This phase of manifestation shifts from confronting obstacles to healing and integration. The Healer allows us to transmute what no longer serves us, rewiring resistance, such as old wounds and limiting beliefs, with empowering new patterns that align with our highest potential.

The Healer's energy is restorative, ensuring that transformation is fully integrated and long-lasting. Her role is to realign our inner foundation by rewiring us from the inside out. By strengthening and redefining our inner landscape to align with the future self we are trying to manifest, allowing our external reality to mirror the growth within.

Without the Healer's influence, unresolved energies and outdated habits linger, making it easy to fall back into self-sabotaging cycles. Neglecting her role keeps us tethered to old beliefs, preventing us from embodying the growth necessary for manifestation to unfold naturally.

Chapter 5 – The Healer Archetype: The Inner Transformer

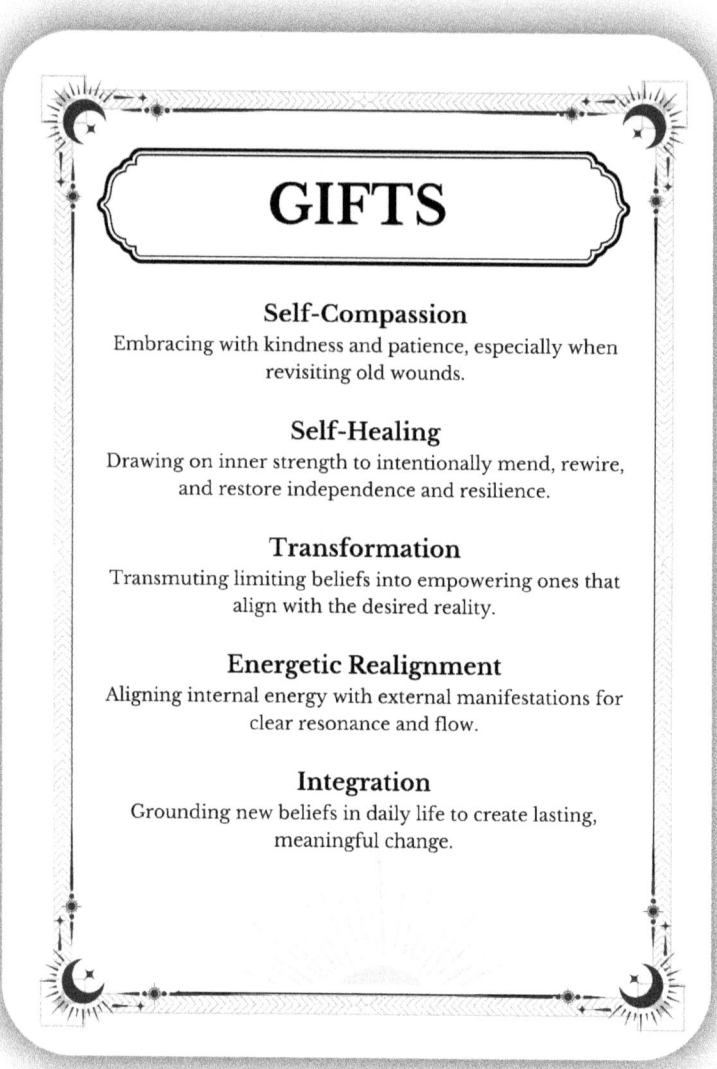

GIFTS

Self-Compassion
Embracing with kindness and patience, especially when revisiting old wounds.

Self-Healing
Drawing on inner strength to intentionally mend, rewire, and restore independence and resilience.

Transformation
Transmuting limiting beliefs into empowering ones that align with the desired reality.

Energetic Realignment
Aligning internal energy with external manifestations for clear resonance and flow.

Integration
Grounding new beliefs in daily life to create lasting, meaningful change.

The deepest wounds, when embraced, become the greatest teachers.

The Inside Players: Master the Manifestation Game

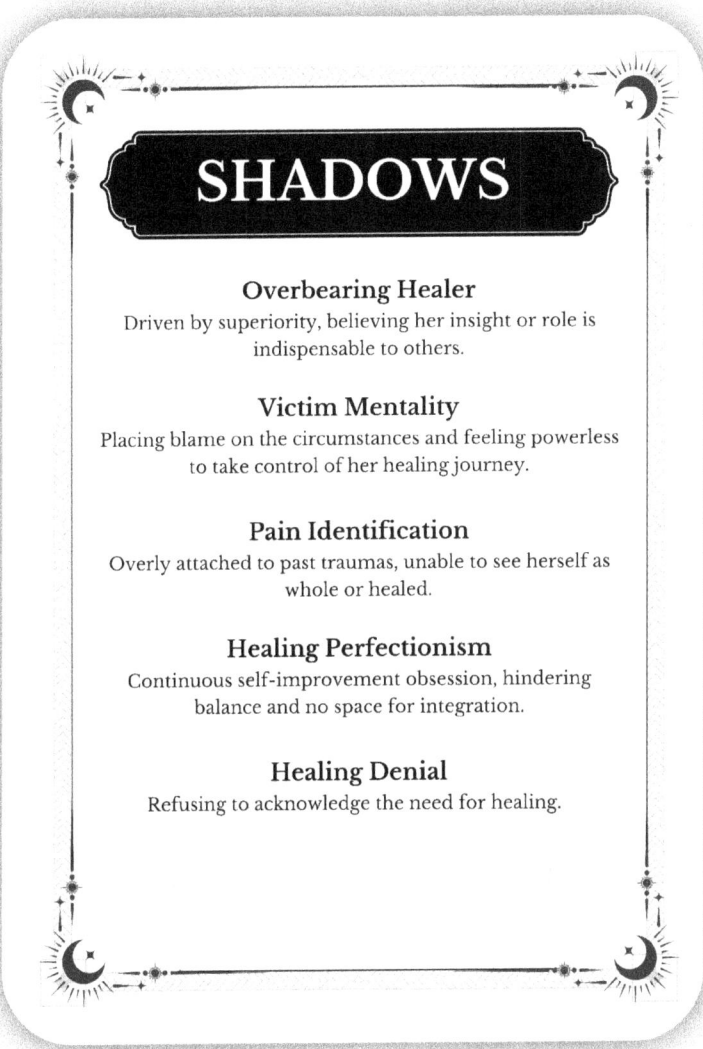

SHADOWS

Overbearing Healer
Driven by superiority, believing her insight or role is indispensable to others.

Victim Mentality
Placing blame on the circumstances and feeling powerless to take control of her healing journey.

Pain Identification
Overly attached to past traumas, unable to see herself as whole or healed.

Healing Perfectionism
Continuous self-improvement obsession, hindering balance and no space for integration.

Healing Denial
Refusing to acknowledge the need for healing.

Pain held too tightly weaves itself into the bones.

Overcoming the Obstacles of the Healer

In the Healer phase, obstacles come from resisting the process of transformation and holding on to old wounds. Without allowing deep healing and release, the energy needed for new manifestations gets trapped in old patterns, preventing forward movement.

Practising Self-Compassion

One of the surprising challenges during the Healer phase is how old wounds we thought fully resolved can resurface unexpectedly. This can lead to shock or frustration. For example, unresolved emotions from a breakup may arise years later, even in the midst of a happy marriage. Rather than dismissing these emotions as irrelevant, they should be recognised as valuable signals to areas that still need healing.

This resurfacing reflects the layered nature of healing, revealing emotions that were previously too overwhelming to process and became accessible over time. Each return to familiar wounds offers a deeper opportunity for growth. The Healer archetype teaches us that healing is a gradual, layered journey, like tending to a garden. By approaching the process with patience and self-compassion, we honour each layer as it arises, preventing overwhelm and allowing time for each shift in our perception and emotion to integrate fully.

> *"Unprocessed emotions often hide in the shadows of our consciousness, awaiting the right moment to be fully released."*

Resurfacing wounds are, therefore, not setbacks but are opportunities to expand consciousness and realign with our true selves. Embracing this process makes healing the foundation for surrendered manifestation, aligning us with greater inner harmony and well-being.

Creating Inner Harmony Through Transformation

Transformation, especially during a powerful period of awakening, can feel like being put into a blender as we are stripped of what no longer serves us. This can leave us feeling raw, vulnerable, and exposed. As familiar parts of ourselves fall away, we may also experience a profound loss or disorientation.

This discomfort can drive us back to old habits, preventing lasting change. The Healer's shadows of victim mentality and identification with pain can further keep us resisting transformation. Even after uncovering deep-rooted limitations, we may cling to familiar patterns that feel safe but limit our growth. This resistance often stems from a subconscious need to hold on to old identities and habits, reinforcing our attachment to what is familiar.

The Healer, in close partnership with the nurturing containment of the Mother, helps us create a sense of safety within change. Together, they help us ground ourselves in this new state, using practices like deep breathing to signal to our nervous system that this path is safe. With the nurturing guidance of the Healer and the Mother, transformation can unfold gently, organically, and beautifully. With this synergistic approach, we realign energetically, gradually restoring inner harmony and reconnecting with our wholeness.

> ### Archetypes in the Healing Process
>
> Healing is a cyclical journey, often requiring us to revisit familiar wounds to process emotions that were once too overwhelming. Through cycles of healing, each archetype contributes a unique energy and quality that deepens our self-awareness, fostering growth and consciously cultivating a life of purpose.
>
> Just as the Maiden needs to approach her boldest dreams with small, manageable steps, the Healer guides us to heal in small, intentional doses.

Chapter 5 – The Healer Archetype: The Inner Transformer

> This is where the Mother creates a nurturing container, holding space for these shifts and allowing us to integrate without feeling overwhelmed.
>
> The Huntress provides that courage and persistence needed to revisit and face challenges, with each return deepening our transformation.
>
> Finally, the Lover enriches the process by encouraging us to embrace each layer of healing with vulnerability, love, presence, and gratitude, fostering self-compassion and lasting transformation.
>
> As our inner world becomes aligned, we are better prepared to embrace a state of receptivity explored in the Queen and to authentically express our truest selves with the Wild Woman.
>
> This conscious alignment reduces the likelihood of subconscious patterns disrupting our resonance and creating misaligned manifestations.

Reinforcing New Patterns

Healing perfectionism creates the obstacle of perpetual self-fixing, where we constantly search for issues to 'fix' rather than allowing new patterns to fully integrate. This cycle can keep us from experiencing true transformation, as each shift remains incomplete and transient without proper reinforcement.

Creating space is only the first step; to solidify the transformation, it must be embedded into daily life. **Neuroplasticity** is key to this process, as it reshapes neural pathways through repeated habits and thoughts. The more we reinforce these pathways, the stronger they become, making transformation more natural and sustainable.

By consciously cultivating positive habits and thought patterns, we can rewire the brain by creating new pathways aligning with our desired outcomes. This adaptability of the brain means that even long-standing habits or beliefs can be changed with consistent effort, enabling lasting personal growth and transformation.

> *"I am not what happened to me, I am what I choose to become."*
>
> — *Carl Jung*

Transformation requires an ongoing commitment. As we integrate new patterns, we move closer to the version of ourselves that already exists in potential. It's in the daily choices—the small, consistent actions, where real change takes root. And while challenges may arise, each moment of reinforcement brings us one step closer to the life we desire. When we commit to this ongoing practice of growth, we not only reshape our minds but also begin to live as the people we are becoming.

From Deep Wounds to Deep Healing

As I peeled back the layers in my healing journey, I created space for deeper patterns to emerge. Among them was a deeply rooted belief passed down by family lineage that shaped not only my experience but also the generations before me.

My grandmother came from a poor, uneducated family and was often looked down upon by my grandfather's relatives. She was his first wife and bore him twelve children. He married a second wife, frequently abandoning my grandmother and the children for long stretches of time with no support. When he did return, it was often to inflict harsh violence on her and the family.

Food was so scarce that the family survived on a small bowl of rice with soy each day. Out of desperation, they once stole a neighbour's chicken, and eating it felt like an extravagant luxury compared to their usual meagre meals.

These experiences shaped my mum's belief that survival depended on relentless hard work, a mindset she passed down to me from a very young age: "You have to work harder than everyone else if you want to survive." For her, life was a constant struggle, where putting food on the table could never be taken for granted.

Naturally, I inherited this belief, which became one of the subconscious layers I unknowingly carried through life. It drove me to push myself relentlessly, convinced that slowing down or relaxing wasn't an option. Life was about survival, and survival meant constant hard work.

Unsurprisingly, this lack of safety showed up as tension in my body in the form of hypervigilance, a constant need to be on the go, and an inability to feel grounded. I often felt like I couldn't rest unless I was performing at my best, which cultivated a relentless type-A personality. My mind was always racing, unable to switch off, exacerbated by undiagnosed ADHD. I overcommitted to tasks, filling my schedule excessively as a way to distract myself from unresolved discomfort, clinging to a false sense of productivity as safety.

To address this, I began consciously rewiring my nervous system, teaching myself that I was no longer bound by the struggles of my ancestors. Hot yoga became my entry point. Its intensity forced me out of my thoughts and mind and into my body, demanding a presence that allowed me to better sense my bodily sensations from which I had become so disconnected. I was finally able to release tension that had been so constant it felt like a part of who I was.

From there, I delved into inner work to map my sympathetic and parasympathetic states. I learned to recognise when I was triggered and consciously guide myself back to safety through mindfulness practices like breathwork. This became a powerful tool for calming my nervous system and anchoring myself in the present. These practices taught me to slow down and find parts of myself I didn't realise existed. Over time, this process became the foundation for deeper transformation, helping me cultivate stillness and embrace rest —not as a threat but as a vital part of thriving.

This new way of being became my normal. Thriving was no longer tied to constant motion or effort but grounded in balance, presence, and trust in my body's wisdom.

Healing with the Support of Others

The **Overbearing Healer** often manifests as the **Savior Complex**, a compulsion to 'save' or 'fix' others. This urge often stems from an upbringing where helping or taking control created a sense of safety. Over time, this can create an identity based on helping others, making it feel like a necessity rather than a choice.

Without healthy boundaries, this dynamic fosters codependence, keeping others reliant rather than encouraging independence. It can also serve as a way to avoid one's own unhealed wounds by focusing on other people's problems instead of addressing personal growth.

This compulsion to 'fix' can result in inflated responsibility—an excessive sense of accountability for events beyond one's control—and assumed authority, where someone believes they have the right to act on behalf of someone else. Both can diminish other people's experiences and make them feel dismissive, for example, when one downplays other people's struggles, implying their own hardships are/were worse or more valid. Statements like "My trauma is worse" may provide

Chapter 5 – The Healer Archetype: The Inner Transformer

fleeting validation, but they reinforce separation, limit empathy, and come from a place of unhealed wounds.

Others may resist seeking support entirely, isolating themselves with the belief that they must handle everything alone or that their struggles aren't significant enough. While self-reliance has its value, over-isolation can hinder access to fresh perspectives and connections that foster deeper healing.

Self-healing is not about fixing others or enduring life in silence; it's about restoring and transforming oneself. By prioritising our healing, we strengthen our foundation and model emotional stability for others, creating a balanced environment that encourages self-reliance and meaningful connection.

From Saviour to Self-Healer

My mum's difficult childhood meant that, as an adult, she lacked many resources to regulate herself. She survived the abuse of her childhood by forming a co-dependent dynamic with her family. In her isolation after relocating to Australia, this resulted in the parentification of her children, where we took on the responsibilities of an adult out of necessity. In turn, this fostered a saviour complex that followed me into adulthood. If I could fix something, I felt I could protect myself from being ambushed by unpredictability. This role became deeply ingrained, as it was tied to my sense of safety.

Trying to change this was challenging because it meant confronting the guilt tied to the confused role I played as a child and the fear that relinquishing it would be unsafe. I needed to do a lot of rewiring to shift this belief. I started with inner child work using journaling and guided meditations to connect with the younger version of myself who carried these burdens. I also practiced visualisation techniques to create a safe space for her and reassured her that she was no longer responsible for everyone else's emotions.

This wasn't a one-time fix but a process I had to revisit many times. Each time, a new belief would surface, or the inner child wouldn't feel fully safe relinquishing her role. Sometimes, it was about releasing just 10% of that responsibility, knowing that healing often happens in layers.

From there, I reframed my sense of responsibility, recognising that fixing others was never my job. I practiced self-reflection exercises and used affirmations like, "I am responsible for myself, not for others," to solidify this understanding. I also learned to protect my empathy, identifying where it was being overextended and setting firm boundaries to prioritise my well-being. Boundary-setting often involved practising assertive communication through role-playing or scripting conversations to feel confident in expressing my needs.

Through this layered process, I redefined my understanding of safety—it didn't depend on fixing others or controlling every situation. I learned to build a relationship with the unpredictability of life, approaching it with resilience and self-compassion. In doing so, I liberated myself from old patterns and stepped into greater alignment with my true self and the life I was ready to create.

Journal Prompts

1. Which parts of my inner landscape feel 'sticky' with outdated stories?
   Reflect on lingering narratives or emotions. Consider how allowing these layers to emerge naturally supports gentle, integrated healing.

2. What lessons have I gained from the patterns I'm ready to release?
   Reflect on insights from these patterns and how they guide you forward, grounding you in wisdom.

3. What qualities do I wish to embody as I move forward?
   Focus on new empowering qualities and what small actions could support the embodiment of them now.

4. In what situations do I take on more than what is my own?
   Reflect on patterns where you assume more responsibility for others' emotions, tasks, or struggles.

5. What gifts have emerged from my healing journey that I can offer to myself or the world?
   Think about the strengths you have developed as a result of your healing process. Consider how these strengths can be seen as a gift for yourself or others.

From Healer to Queen

As the Healer completes her work of transformation, the Queen now rises, ready to claim her sovereignty and worthiness to receive. With the internal work done, the Queen steps into her power, fully embodying the confidence and authority needed to receive abundance.

CHAPTER 6
The Queen Archetype: The Worthy Receiver

"You are a divine being. You matter; you count. You come from realms of unimaginable power and light, and you will return to those realms."

—Terence McKenna

The Queen embodies sovereignty and worthiness within the manifestation process. Building on the foundation laid by the previous Sacred Feminine archetypes, she steps forward with unwavering authority, fully grounded in her self-worth.

This phase represents pure receptivity, where manifestation flows effortlessly through surrender, not striving. The Queen trusts the universe to serve her, releasing the need to control outcomes. She knows what is meant for her will arrive in its own time. With grace and openness, she invites abundance to flow naturally into her life.

The Queen's energy radiates calm confidence and sovereign presence, rooted in the truth that worthiness is intrinsic. She reminds us there is no need to hustle or chase what is already ours. By embracing her sovereignty, we step into a state of graceful receptivity, where abundance becomes a natural extension of our being. This is the essence of surrendered manifestation: allowing the flow of life to align seamlessly with our intentions.

Chapter 6 – The Queen Archetype: The Worthy Receiver

Resisting the Queen's influence leads to cycles of over-effort and control, creating internal resistance and blocking abundance. Without her self-assured presence, we may feel compelled to prove our value, disconnecting from the ease and flow that true worthiness offers. By aligning with the Queen, we release these struggles and welcome abundance with grace and certainty.

The Inside Players: Master the Manifestation Game

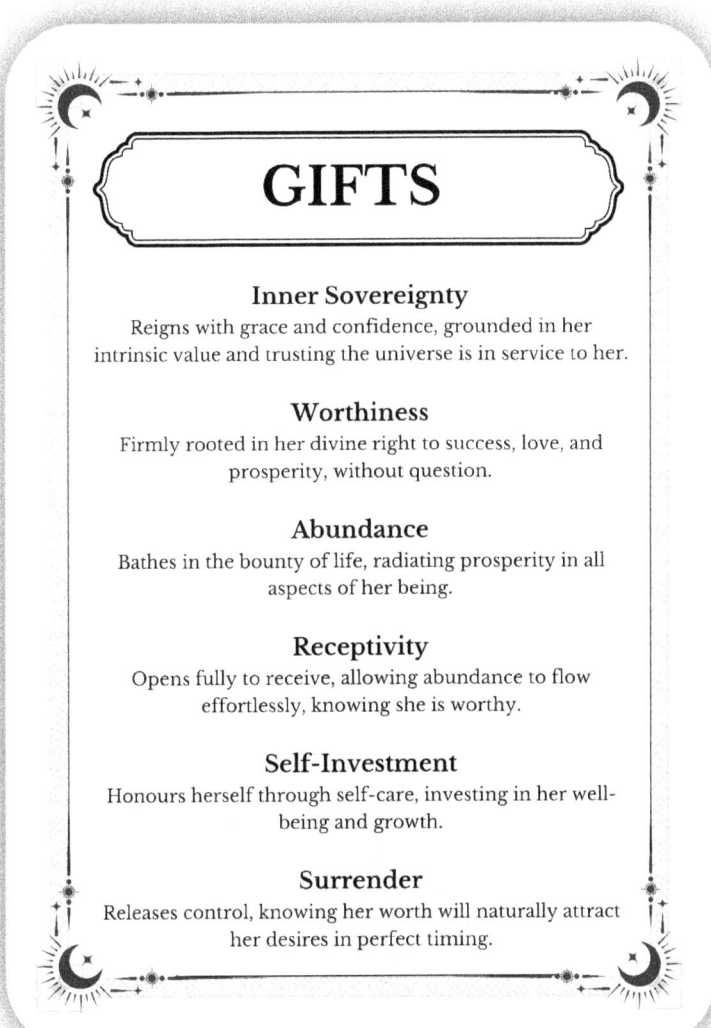

GIFTS

Inner Sovereignty
Reigns with grace and confidence, grounded in her intrinsic value and trusting the universe is in service to her.

Worthiness
Firmly rooted in her divine right to success, love, and prosperity, without question.

Abundance
Bathes in the bounty of life, radiating prosperity in all aspects of her being.

Receptivity
Opens fully to receive, allowing abundance to flow effortlessly, knowing she is worthy.

Self-Investment
Honours herself through self-care, investing in her well-being and growth.

Surrender
Releases control, knowing her worth will naturally attract her desires in perfect timing.

Sovereignty is not claimed—it is remembered.

Chapter 6 – The Queen Archetype: The Worthy Receiver

SHADOWS

Unclaimed Sovereignty
Fails to recognise her own authority, deferring power to external forces.

Unworthiness
Doubts her value, questioning her right to receive and blocking flow.

Scarcity Mindset
Perceives life as limited, clinging tightly to resources and opportunities, and unable to embrace abundance.

Entitlement
Expects results without personal growth or effort, confusing self-worth with demands for control.

Over-Control
Driven by fear of inadequacy, she resists flow by trying to control outcomes.

One who denies their own worth will chase what was meant to be received.

Overcoming the Obstacles of the Queen

The Queen's core challenge lies in doubting her inherent worth, which can manifest as a need for control or resistance to receiving. By reclaiming her sovereignty and trusting her right to abundance, she allows her manifestations to flow with grace and ease.

Your Innate Worthiness to Receive

Unworthiness often manifests as low self-esteem and difficulty receiving—whether it's love, support, abundance, or even compliments. For the Queen, this manifests as hesitation to claim her throne, doubting her right to lead with confidence and grace. Past experiences or a vague sense of inadequacy can create barriers, blocking the flow of support and abundance.

Imposter syndrome is another form of this doubt, driving a constant need to prove oneself despite achievements. This self-doubt keeps the Queen from ruling with trust in her inner authority.

True worthiness, however, is intrinsic and cannot be earned or validated by others. When the Queen stands in her sovereignty, trusting her inherent value, she opens the gates to abundance, allowing life to reflect her confidence and alignment.

> *"You alone are the judge of your worth and your goal is to discover infinite worth in yourself, no matter what anyone else thinks."*

By reclaiming her worth, the Queen becomes a sovereign force, commanding life's gifts to flow freely and elevating her entire kingdom.

Chapter 6 – The Queen Archetype: The Worthy Receiver

Bathing in Prosperity

Another cause of difficulty in receiving is an underlying feeling of guilt or shame around abundance—whether it manifests as, for example, material wealth, health and wellness, emotional support or relationships, time for oneself, or personal fulfilment. This guilt can be especially triggered when those close to us foster feelings of unworthiness over success. Comments like, "You've got it all," can make us feel as though our abundance is unfair or selfish, particularly when friends or family are less fortunate.

Cultural conditioning can teach us that sacrificing is virtuous and that receiving too much is selfish. Some spiritual beliefs also reinforce the idea that suffering is noble and that one must earn abundance by enduring hardship or 'paying off' karmic debt.

This guilt is related to the scarcity mindset, where we feel we don't have permission to live abundantly while others are suffering. The Queen, however, knows that her abundance does not take away from anyone else's. She understands that there is enough for everyone and that by receiving fully, she can give more freely. She embodies the truth that abundance is limitless; in fact, her prosperity creates more for others.

Transforming Scarcity into Inspiration

Scarcity mindset often reveals itself as jealousy or envy. For the Queen, this can manifest as a fear of losing her position or power, creating the belief that life is a 'zero-sum game' where another's success diminishes her own. Instead of finding inspiration in others' achievements, she may see them as threats, fostering separation and self-doubt. This drains her energy and distracts her from channelling it into building her realm or nurturing her own growth.

Entitlement, on the other hand, may emerge as the belief that the Queen's position guarantees success without effort or self-reflection.

This mindset focuses on outcomes rather than the journey, leading to dissatisfaction when expectations aren't met. It can also create comparisons, where one feels deserving of what others have achieved without recognising the work or growth involved.

Both scarcity and entitlement hinder the Queen from embodying true sovereignty, blocking her openness to receive and limiting her ability to see opportunities beyond a narrow definition of success.

True empowerment for the Queen comes from accountability and self-investment. By directing her energy toward personal growth, learning, and self-care, she reaffirms her readiness to receive abundance. This shift strengthens her inner authority, aligning her with the understanding that abundance is an internal state—one that naturally attracts prosperity and fulfilment.

When the Queen embraces this perspective, the success of others no longer feels threatening. Instead, it serves as an inspiration and a reflection of her potential. In this state of sovereignty, success becomes a collective journey rather than a competition; achievements contribute to shared growth and uplift the entire kingdom.

> The peak of personal growth is self-actualisation, where we realise our full potential. At its core is the **Law of Circulation**, the principle that what we put out into the world energetically is returned to us. It is a declaration of worth to invest time, money, or effort in ourselves, inviting the universe to respond in kind.

Remembering Your Sovereignty

The Queen's attempts to maintain security by tightly managing every detail of life can result in over-controlling. This instinct reflects an underlying struggle with trust, not only in life's natural flow but also in her ability to rule with confidence. While this vigilance may feel protective, it brings rigidity that limits openness to unexpected opportunities aligned with her highest intentions. The more she micromanages outcomes, the harder it becomes to relax, release, and embody the ease essential to surrendered manifestation.

At its root, this need for control reveals a gap in self-trust. Rather than leading from her inner authority, the Queen may focus outward, trying to manage every aspect of her realm. This reflects a lack of faith in her innate worthiness to receive life's support. This shadow traps her in a cycle of relentless effort, disconnected from the balance and grace that allow true manifestation.

Reclaiming her sovereignty means releasing the need to control and returning to her inner strength. By aligning with life's natural flow, she reconnects with her power, inviting abundance and creating a life that reflects her highest intentions. In surrendering control, the Queen leads with wisdom and opens her kingdom to limitless possibilities.

Recognising the Worthiness to Receive

The Queen shadow of unworthiness was clearly present in my mum's life. She worked tirelessly to provide for her three children while managing her beauty therapy business. Despite her devotion to family and work, she often said things like, "I don't have time to care for myself" or "I can't afford to spend money on myself."

These statements reflected a sense of pride, and working hard and sacrificing her own needs became a badge of honour. However, beneath this was a more painful truth: the belief that she wasn't worthy of receiving.

This was evident in both subtle and significant ways. Even when she was physically injured, such as when she hurt her back, she refused to take proper care of herself. She would continue to move heavy objects around the house, for example, despite being in pain. When we offered to help, she would insist, "No, it's too heavy; you might hurt yourself!"

It was as if her own pain didn't matter, but the idea of us getting hurt was unacceptable. The message she sent, whether knowingly or not, was that it was okay for her to endure discomfort, but not us.

This refusal to accept help or to pause and rest was deeply tied to her sense of worth. She gave endlessly to others but couldn't allow herself to receive even the care and support she so clearly needed. Her life experiences had reinforced the idea that nurturing and rest were luxuries she didn't deserve. When life repeatedly reflects hardship, it's easy to believe that that's all there is.

My mum's experience is a prime example of how our circumstances can shape our beliefs and how we can lose sight of our innate worth.

The shadow my mum faced was the belief that her worth was tied solely to giving, working hard, and sacrificing while viewing self-care and receiving as luxuries that she didn't feel worthy of. This mindset created a barrier to accepting help, rest, and care, even when she needed them most. By basing her value on what she could give to others, she struggled to reclaim her sovereignty and honour her own needs.

The Queen archetype reminds us that true sovereignty lies in recognising our inherent worth. The gift my mum couldn't fully claim was the ability to receive without guilt or feeling undeserving. Had she embraced this balance, she might have found greater ease and fulfilment, allowing herself to receive as much as she gave.

Chapter 6 – The Queen Archetype: The Worthy Receiver

Journal Prompts

1. What conditions do I set for myself to allow myself to receive?
   Consider any standards or achievements you feel you must reach before allowing yourself to feel truly deserving of abundance.

2. How comfortable am I with receiving support and abundance?
   Explore any resistance or discomfort you experience when accepting help or embracing abundance in your life.

3. Where might I be micromanaging outcomes that suffocate my ability to receive?
   Reflect on where you might be holding on too tightly and why you need to manage every detail.

4. What qualities do I admire in others that I want to cultivate within myself?
   Identify traits that inspire you and reflect on how embodying them could expand your opportunities.

5. How do I feel when others succeed, and what does this reveal about my relationship with abundance?
   Notice your reactions to others' success and what they may reveal about your relationship with abundance.

From Queen to Wild Woman

The Queen stands in her worth, holding the space for abundance to arrive. Her confidence in what she deserves is unshakable, a reflection of her inner sovereignty. With her role fulfilled, we can now step into the realm of the Wild Woman, who is guided not by rules but by the deep, primal instincts of our truest expression.

CHAPTER 7
The Wild Woman Archetype: The Authentic Liberator

"When you let go of who you think you are, you become who you were meant to be."

—*Taoist Proverb*

THE WILD WOMAN is the final sacred feminine archetype and embodies unapologetic authenticity and primal truth. After grounding our worth through the Queen, the Wild Woman calls us to renounce societal conditioning and embrace our primal identity, manifesting from a place of liberation.

In this phase, manifestation becomes an act of deep alignment with our soul's true nature. Here, we move from seeking external approval to embodying radical self-honesty. The Wild Woman guides us to shatter the expectations and conditioning that dilute our authenticity and reconnect with the unmasked self, free of the more superficial identities we wear for the world. Only by honouring this pure essence can we manifest desires that resonate with our soul's purpose.

The Wild Woman's energy radiates raw, unfiltered self-expression—untamed and unapologetic. She calls us to strip away the layers of fear, judgement, and conformity that suppress our true essence, reclaiming the authentic self that lies beneath. With her influence, we find the courage to embrace forgotten aspects of ourselves and reconnect with parts of ourselves long silenced, honouring and integrating them into our mainstream life. Through this reclamation, we discover the path to manifestation that is uniquely aligned with who we truly are at our core.

When we resist the call of the Wild Woman, we risk losing ourselves in conformity, bound by societal expectations and self-imposed restrictions. This disconnect leads us to ignore our deepest desires and confine ourselves within the limits of what is 'safe' and 'acceptable.' Without her influence, we forsake the richness of soul-aligned living, limiting our potential to fulfil our calling. Embracing the Wild Woman liberates us to manifest a life aligned with our wild, unbroken spirit.

The Inside Players: Master the Manifestation Game

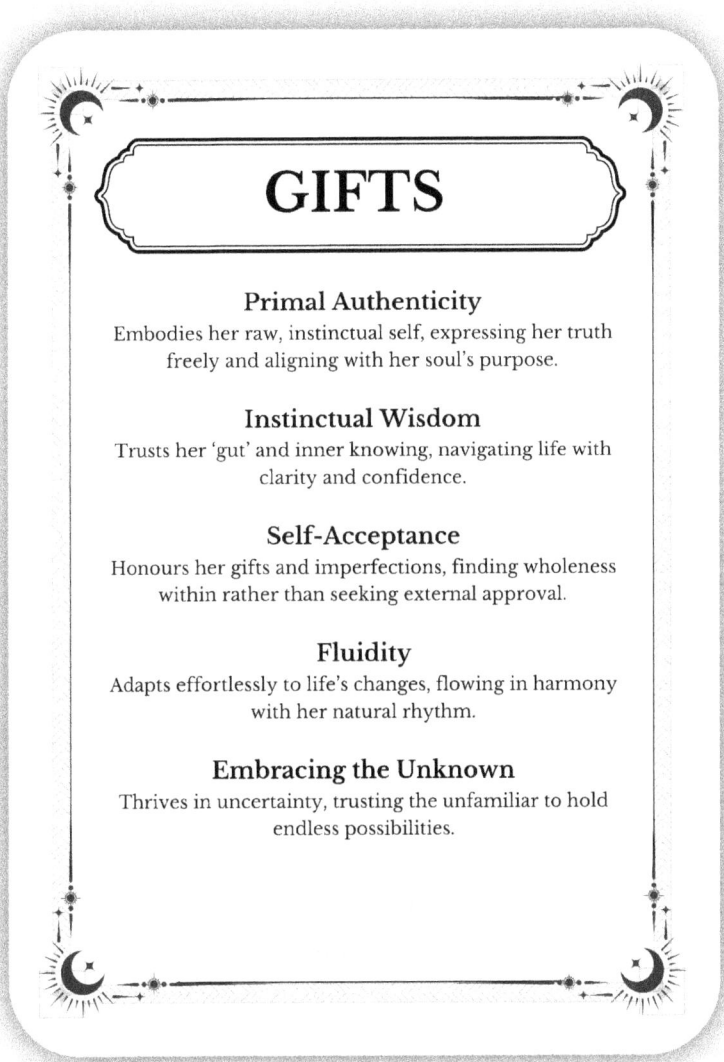

GIFTS

Primal Authenticity
Embodies her raw, instinctual self, expressing her truth freely and aligning with her soul's purpose.

Instinctual Wisdom
Trusts her 'gut' and inner knowing, navigating life with clarity and confidence.

Self-Acceptance
Honours her gifts and imperfections, finding wholeness within rather than seeking external approval.

Fluidity
Adapts effortlessly to life's changes, flowing in harmony with her natural rhythm.

Embracing the Unknown
Thrives in uncertainty, trusting the unfamiliar to hold endless possibilities.

A wild river does not seek permission to carve mountains.

Chapter 7 – The Wild Woman Archetype: The Authentic Liberator

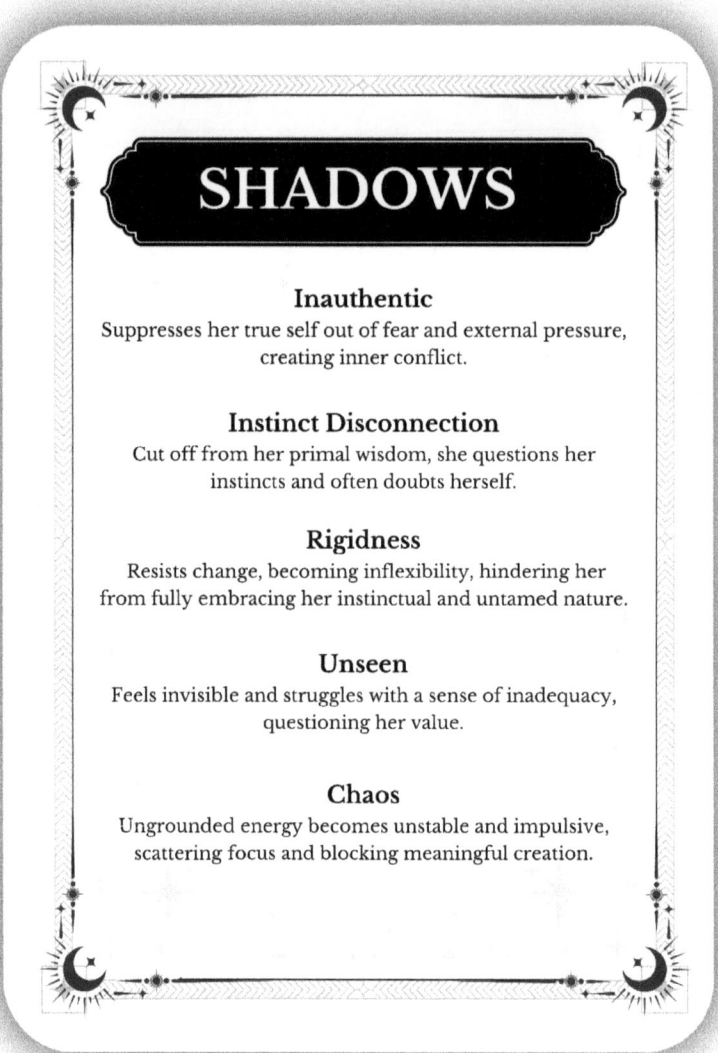

SHADOWS

Inauthentic
Suppresses her true self out of fear and external pressure, creating inner conflict.

Instinct Disconnection
Cut off from her primal wisdom, she questions her instincts and often doubts herself.

Rigidity
Resists change, becoming inflexibility, hindering her from fully embracing her instinctual and untamed nature.

Unseen
Feels invisible and struggles with a sense of inadequacy, questioning her value.

Chaos
Ungrounded energy becomes unstable and impulsive, scattering focus and blocking meaningful creation.

A wild heart bound too long forgets how to run.

Overcoming the Obstacles of the Wild Woman

The Wild Woman faces obstacles when she suppresses her instinctual nature due to societal conditioning or fear of judgement. Disconnection from her wildness and intuition disrupts the manifestation process, preventing her from fully aligning with her true desires.

Reclaiming Your Authenticity

From an early age, society conditions us to conform, teaching us to suppress our natural instincts and wildness to fit into what is deemed acceptable by our families, schools, and broader culture. The desire to belong and avoid judgment often leads us to mute our raw emotions, instincts, and energy, creating a deep-rooted fear of rejection. Being 'too much' or stepping outside the norm feels risky, as it might invite exclusion or criticism.

> *"To be yourself in a world that is constantly trying to make you something else is the greatest accomplishment."*
>
> —*Ralph Waldo Emerson*

As children in the Maiden phase, we are naturally expressive, creative, and open to possibility. The need to fit in gradually leads us to abandon these qualities, dimming the bright curiosity and freedom characterising the Maiden. Over time, we also lose touch with the instincts and untamed expression of the Wild Woman, which are essential for authentic manifestation.

This self-suppression creates an inner conflict, hindering our ability to express ourselves authentically and leading to self-doubt. Disconnected from our true purpose, we struggle to manifest with clarity and conviction. The Wild Woman challenges this by urging us to reclaim the parts of ourselves we've buried, encouraging us to embrace our untamed energy, instincts, and desires, allowing us to manifest a life that truly reflects our soul's essence.

Chapter 7 – The Wild Woman Archetype: The Authentic Liberator

Self-Hatred to Self-Acceptance

When The Wild Woman feels unseen, this often leads to feelings of being misunderstood and invisible. She may feel that she doesn't fit in or that her true self isn't welcome. Over time, this isolation fuels an internal struggle, planting the seeds of self-doubt and turning frustrations inward. Many of us begin to believe that our authentic self is unworthy or unacceptable, driving self-sabotage and preventing us from fully embracing our unique gifts.

As this disconnection intensifies, self-criticism takes root, leading to self-hatred and a rejection of parts of ourselves as flawed or inadequate. The pain of feeling unseen creates an internal polarisation, sparking cycles of shame and self-rejection. When left ungrounded, this inner turmoil can erupt into chaotic, self-destructive patterns—volatile and erratic behaviours that derail our ability to focus and disrupt surrendered manifestation.

By embracing all parts of ourselves, we move from feeling misunderstood to fully honouring our true selves. The greatest power lies in cultivating self-acceptance from within, liberating us from the need for external validation. This inner freedom allows us to rekindle the Wild Woman's unapologetic authenticity and create from a place of wholeness and true alignment.

Reconnecting with Instinctual Wisdom

For centuries, the instinct—the heart of the Wild Woman's manifestation process—has been marginalised by societal conditioning. Since the Age of Enlightenment (late 17th to early 19th century), society has increasingly prioritised logic, reason, and measurable outcomes *(yang, linear)*. At the same time, instinct *(yin, non-linear)* has been dismissed as unreliable or even irrational due to its subjective nature. This cultural shift has led us to trust external validation and structured thinking over our own deeply rooted, instinctive knowing.

Instinct operates through tracking subtle cues—physical sensations, gut feelings, and emotional responses—that bypass logical analysis.

These cues, while immeasurable, are vital for aligned decision-making. **Dual-process theory** supports this view, showing that our minds process information through two systems that roughly correspond to instinct and logic. System 1 is instinctive, fast, and automatic, and System 2 is deliberate, rational, and slow. While society has often favoured the rational System 2, System 1—our instincts—offers the deep, grounded wisdom that the Wild Woman invites us to reclaim.

> Recent research has also shown that System 1 cognitive processing, although intuitive and automatic, is not fixed and is improved with experience and feedback so that an 'expert intuition' can develop over time. For example, the swift moves of a chess master or expert surgeon.

When disconnected from our primal wisdom, we doubt our inner guidance and become vulnerable to external influences. This self-doubt fractures our ability to act authentically, leaving us reliant on the perspectives of others and disconnected from our true path.

Reclaiming our instincts reconnects us to the primal wisdom of the Wild Woman, awakening our untamed essence and the freedom to walk our truest path. By trusting this inner compass, we align with our soul's deepest desires, manifesting authentically and without fear of losing control.

The Gift of Fluidity

One of the most common obstacles in manifestation is not being able to let go of pursuits that no longer serve us. Whether it's a faded relationship, an uninspiring university course, or a successful career that feels unfulfilling, we often feel trapped by the time and energy we've already invested. This psychological trap is the **Sunk-cost fallacy**. It stems from an attachment to past investments; we stay on a path not because it serves us now but because we fear 'wasting' what we've already given.

Holding on to outdated paths restricts growth and blocks the flow of new opportunities that resonate with our evolving desires. For the Wild

Woman, this resistance arises from suppressing her truth. True freedom comes not from clinging to what once was but boldly embracing change and stepping into the unknown. It is an act of honouring the wisdom gained through experience rather than perceiving it as a failure.

> *"Like water, she knows that staying confined in a rigid vessel blocks her flow. She is the river, moving freely with the current of life, releasing what no longer serves her to continue her true path."*

The Wild Woman embodies the wisdom of fluidity and spontaneity, stripping away the constructs that confine our individuality. With the grounded containment provided by the Mother and the inner work cultivated through earlier archetypes, the Wild Woman feels safe enough to break free, rediscovering raw authenticity and untamed self-expression.

Welcoming the Unknown

The fear of uncertainty challenges the Wild Woman's ability to fully embrace freedom, creating tension between the desire for liberation and the comfort of the familiar. Clinging to stability may offer temporary relief but ultimately limits growth and fulfilment.

We've all experienced moments when life didn't go as planned—a relationship ended, a job opportunity was lost—only to later realise these shifts guided us to something better. The Wild Woman invites us to reframe unpredictability, showing us that the unknown is not a threat but an opening to new possibilities.

Surrendered manifestation requires trusting life's unfolding process, even when the unknown feels unsettling or threatening. For the Wild Woman, unpredictability is no threat; it is a source of power. She teaches us to find freedom in the unknown, using life's unexpected turns as fuel for bold, creative, soul-aligned creation. When we release the need for control and trust life's rhythm, true flow emerges, often leading to outcomes far greater than we could have envisioned.

From Misalignment to True Self

Earlier in the book, I shared how I felt my soul slipping away in a job that no longer served me. I had uprooted my life, moved countries, and invested so much into this role that leaving the job felt like a failure. I found myself jumping between two extremes of cognitive dissonance. On the one hand, I'd zone out, fantasising about a life where I felt free and fulfilled. In those moments, I could almost taste the possibilities of alignment. But then, reality would snap me back, and I'd berate myself for daydreaming. *You should be more committed*, I'd think. *You've worked so hard for this, don't quit now.*

The guilt was relentless. If I wasn't fully invested in the job, wasn't I failing? Shouldn't I be more 'all in?' I kept gaslighting myself, reinforcing the belief that persistence was the key to success. "Winners don't quit," I told myself, conditioning myself to push through discomfort. I clung to the job out of fear—fear of letting people down, fear of wasting what I'd invested, and fear of stepping into the unknown.

Trapped in this sunk cost fallacy, I kept pushing forward on the 'safe' path, believing discomfort was part of the process. In fact, it was a signal that I was disconnected from my inner compass and clinging to a path that no longer aligned with who I was.

The Wild Woman archetype teaches that instincts are a powerful inner guide. Ignoring mine left me stuck in a cycle of guilt and self-reprimanding.

The real challenge wasn't about proving I had grit but confronting my fear of uncertainty and learning to trust the unknown. When I finally acknowledged this, I realised my fear wasn't about quitting but about stepping into the unknown without guarantees. The fantasies I had dismissed as distractions weren't meaningless; they were glimpses of my deeper truth, showing me the way back to alignment.

Letting go wasn't easy, but it had to happen. I stopped seeing discomfort as a challenge to push through and started recognising it as a signal to pivot. Slowly, I built a relationship with uncertainty, not as chaos but as a doorway to growth.

The Wild Woman teaches us that when we release what no longer serves us, we make space for what truly belongs.

Journal Prompts

1. Where in my life am I restraining myself?
   Reflect on areas where you're holding back and not fully embracing your potential.

2. Which parts of myself have I hidden to avoid rejection?
   Think about the aspects of yourself you've suppressed and how allowing them to resurface could bring greater authenticity.

3. What dreams or desires have I put aside to meet the expectations of others?
   Consider any aspirations you may have buried to fit into others' ideas of success or acceptance.

4. When do I feel most alive and true to myself?
   Identify the moments, places, or activities that connect you to your truest essence.

5. In what ways do I trust or ignore my instincts, and how can I deepen that trust?
   Take time to examine your relationship with your inner voice and explore ways to deepen your connection to it.

Completing the Inward Journey

The Wild Woman empowers us to remove layers of conditioning and expectations, freeing us to live in full, unapologetic alignment with our soul's truth. As she closes the Sacred Feminine journey, she reminds us that true authenticity creates a fertile ground for aligned action. In this newfound authenticity, we are ready to step beyond the inner realms and out into the world with courage and purpose.

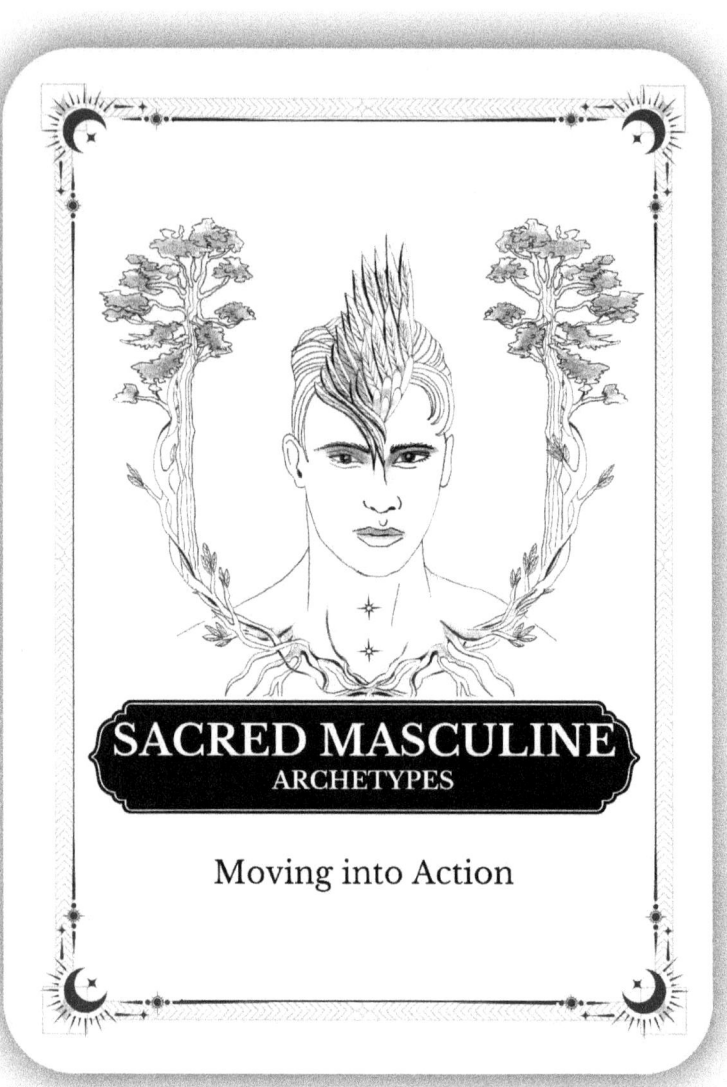

Sacred Masculine Archetypes: Moving into Action

With the Sacred Feminine journey complete, we have grounded in our higher dreams by cultivating a foundation of alignment. This inner work has prepared us to bring our vision into reality, guided now by the Sacred Masculine archetypes.

In the following chapters, we will explore:

- The King
- The Magician
- The Sage

While the Sacred Feminine nurtures and aligns, the Sacred Masculine brings structure, purpose, and directed action, translating inner resonance into real-world creation. Together, they balance being and doing and receiving and creating, completing the cycle of manifestation.

CHAPTER 8
The King Archetype: The Powerful Leader

"The more you align with your true nature, the more powerful your actions become."

—Deepak Chopra

THE KING ARCHETYPE embodies the power of aligned action, transforming inner clarity into purposeful results in the external world. Once inner alignment is established, the King leads us to channel time, energy, and resources into deliberate and structured actions that bring visions to life.

In this phase, manifestation shifts from inner clarity to strategic execution, harmonising values with practical steps. The King's energy embodies structure, coherence, and grounded authority, enabling dreams to flourish through intentional planning and leadership.

While the Queen's sovereignty lies in her intrinsic self-worth, the King represents sovereign power *in action*. However, his leadership is rooted in utilising personal power as a source to create balance and structure, not dominance. Each action aligns with the greater vision, fuelling progress that serves both personal growth and the collective good.

Without the King's balanced influence, actions can become unfocused or overly forceful, leading to burnout and a stalled manifestation process. By engaging the King's wisdom, we shift from reactive effort to intentional, aligned steps where less is more.

Chapter 8 – The King Archetype: The Powerful Leader

GIFTS

Sovereign Power
Claiming personal power, wielding it responsibly with integrity, balanced authority with purpose.

Servitude
Leads selflessly, empowering others for the greater good, without sacrificing integrity for personal gain.

Aligned Action
Knows when to act or pause, taking strategic, intentional steps with stability.

Empowered Delegation
Trusts others to advance the vision, focusing on purpose without micromanaging.

Protective
Establishes firm boundaries to shield values and vision from external interference.

True power builds, it does not break; it lifts, it does not take.

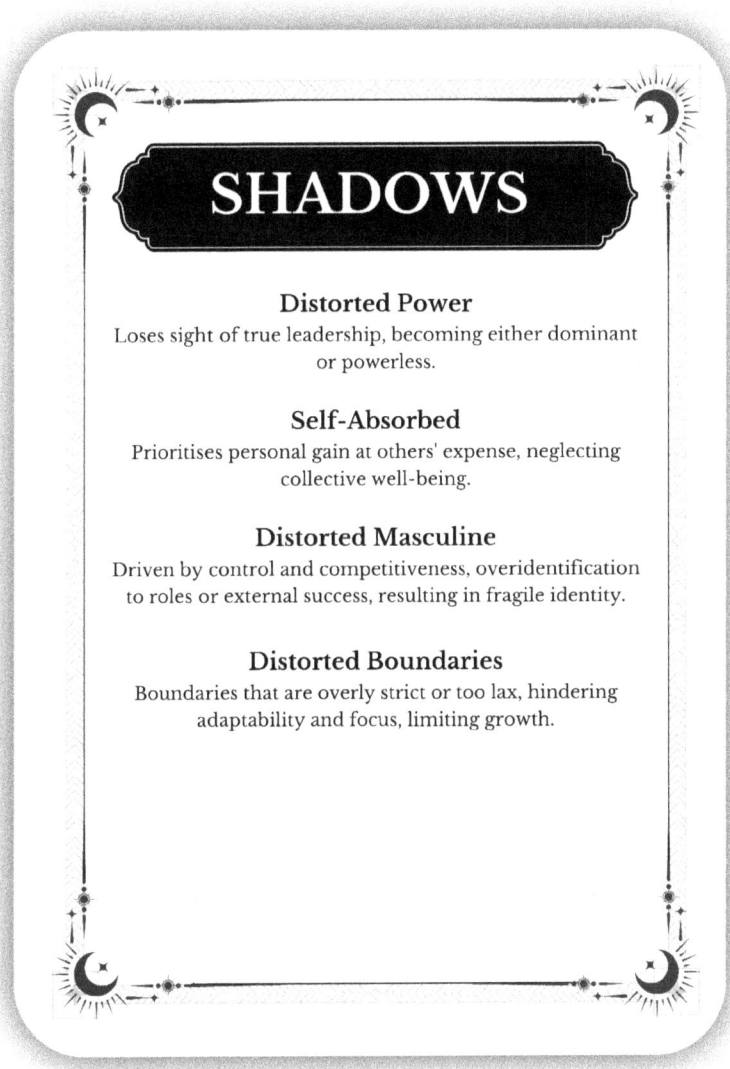

SHADOWS

Distorted Power
Loses sight of true leadership, becoming either dominant or powerless.

Self-Absorbed
Prioritises personal gain at others' expense, neglecting collective well-being.

Distorted Masculine
Driven by control and competitiveness, overidentification to roles or external success, resulting in fragile identity.

Distorted Boundaries
Boundaries that are overly strict or too lax, hindering adaptability and focus, limiting growth.

A kingdom led by fear is a prison of its own making.

Overcoming the Obstacles of the King

At the core of these obstacles lies a distorted masculine energy, driven by the need for control and focused on relentless effort and the misuse of power. This imbalance prioritises forceful action over alignment and trust, disrupting the natural flow of surrendered manifestation. The King restores balance by wielding power with sovereignty, guiding purposeful actions that align with his true purpose.

Reclaiming Sovereign Power

Navigating power dynamics is one of the greatest challenges within the King archetype. Distorted masculine energy often equates power with control, resulting in two extremes: domination, where authority is misused to assert control, or inadequacy, where personal power is surrendered out of self-doubt. These patterns create inner conflict, either through self-limitation or inauthentic leadership.

Many of us have felt the impact of these dynamics, such as when someone's need to assert dominance left us feeling diminished or when hesitation stopped us from stepping into our own authority. Both responses stem from fear or insecurity and disrupt alignment with purpose. The King archetype challenges us to examine how we relate to power, moving beyond reactive behaviours to embody leadership rooted in trust rather than force.

The Types of Power

Power takes many forms, influencing how we connect with ourselves, others, and the world. These dynamics shape our manifestation process, often mirroring internalised beliefs about worth, control, and connection. By understanding the types of power, we can identify where imbalances may exist and how they affect our ability to lead and align with our goals.

Here are the key types of power (also see **Table 4** for examples):

- **Global Rank:** Authority and influence on a global scale, shaping policies and actions that affect entire populations.

- **Local Rank**: Authority within a community or localised area, influencing decisions and norms at a smaller scale.
- **Financial Power**: Wealth grants access to resources and opportunities, often creating imbalances.
- **Cultural and Racial Power**: Privileges linked to cultural or racial identity affect perception and treatment.
- **Gender Power**: Societal norms tied to gender impact authority and resource access.
- **Knowledge Power**: Education or expertise often commands authority and trust.
- **Physical Power**: Physical presence or appearance can influence how authority is perceived.
- **Relational Power**: Social connections and charisma open doors to influence and resources.
- **Age Power**: Authority or biases connected to age, with assumptions about ability or wisdom.

Table 4 High and Low Power Ranks.

Type of Power	High Rank (Example)	Low Rank (Example)
Global Rank	A global celebrity influencing trends worldwide	A local performer with a small, niche audience
Local Rank	A boss in a workplace with authority over decisions	An entry-level employee with limited decision-making power
Financial Power	A wealthy person influencing community projects	Someone with limited finances, whose ideas may be undervalued
Cultural/Racial Power	Majority cultural group members benefiting from systemic privileges	Minority group members facing biases or limitations in resources
Gender Power	Men holding decision-making power in traditional settings	Women or non-binary individuals with limited access to roles
Knowledge Power	An expert with recognised credentials commanding authority	A less formally educated individual, despite practical experience
Physical Power	A healthy, physically fit person being seen as capable or strong	Someone with visible disabilities whose capabilities are dismissed
Relational Power	A charismatic individual who naturally attracts attention	A shy person who often goes unnoticed
Age Power	An older person whose experience is valued	Young person dismissed for inexperience Elderly person overlooked for assumed limitations

Understanding these types of power helps us expose unconscious patterns that lead to misalignment. For example, privilege within certain power dynamics can perpetuate inequities, while marginalisation can create internalised limitations. But both can disrupt our ability to lead with clarity and manifest effectively.

Power Dynamics and Unconscious Biases

Unconscious biases (see **Table 2** on page 65) subtly shape how we perceive and wield power, influencing whether we overcontrol or hesitate to claim authority. For instance:

- **Overcontrol**: Misusing authority to dominate and mask insecurity, such as a manager micromanaging their team because they overvalue their decision-making.

- **Disempowerment**: Reluctance to claim personal power, often internalised through societal stereotypes, such as a team member believing they lack the qualifications to speak up.

These biases distort perception and create resistance by reinforcing fear-based behaviours, such as overcompensating with control or shrinking back from responsibility. By reflecting on how these patterns shape our actions—"Am I masking insecurity with control?" or "Am I diminishing my own authority?"—we can shift towards intentional, aligned leadership.

Power Dynamics and Privilege

Privilege plays a crucial role in how we navigate power and align with our intentions. When left unchecked, privilege can foster exclusionary behaviours, such as prioritising self-interest or ignoring the needs of others. For example, financial privilege might lead someone to dominate decision-making, stifling collaboration and shared growth. Conversely, marginalisation can create internalised doubts, causing hesitation, self-limitation, and a reluctance to take inspired action.

Privilege also often creates blind spots. Those shielded from certain biases may assume their perspective is universal, overlooking the challenges others face. This lack of awareness can hinder alignment by ignoring diverse viewpoints. For those who face systemic bias, these challenges can feel deeply personal, leading to hesitation in sharing their voice or pursuing their goals.

Overcoming these dynamics begins with self-awareness. By reflecting on how privilege and bias shape our actions, we can align more closely with our values, foster collaboration, and create environments where growth is shared. This approach strengthens our ability to manifest authentically while supporting collective abundance.

Sovereign Power Through Servitude

The King archetype teaches that true power lies in using personal agency to create environments of integrity, safety, and shared growth.

Chapter 8 – The King Archetype: The Powerful Leader

When power is rooted in service to others, it fosters collective success and allows manifestation to unfold naturally and expansively.

However, our relationship with authority can become distorted. Fear or insecurity may lead to domination and self-interest or feelings of inadequacy or marginalisation that can cause us to surrender our power, leaving us disconnected from our agency.

> *"While others search for what they can take, a true king searches for what he can give. Everything you see exists together in a delicate balance; as king, you need to understand that balance."*
>
> —*The Lion King*

At its highest expression, the King archetype leads by empowering others, using authority to create pathways for collective growth. At this level, leadership is no longer about control but cultivating an environment of aligned actions where both the individual and the collective can thrive.

Protecting and Elevating Energy

Setting boundaries is essential for protecting energy, maintaining focus, and recognising when relationships or environments no longer support growth. While the Mother archetype preserves inner resources, the King focuses on external commitments, ensuring they align with his purpose and vision. His boundaries are not tools of control but intentional acts of clarity, protection, and alignment.

For the Sacred Masculine, boundaries are more than just saying "no." They are a conscious commitment to safeguarding energy, creating external frameworks that foster growth and amplify his leadership. By intentionally letting go of relationships or environments that no longer align, the King opens space for opportunities that support expansion and cultivates connections that magnify his vision and purpose.

The Inside Players: Master the Manifestation Game

> *"Boundaries are the distance at which I can love you and me simultaneously."*
>
> —*Prentis Hemphill*

The King's boundaries are not restrictive—they are empowering. They reflect his commitment to protect what matters most while channelling energy towards what uplifts himself and the collective. Boundaries are the frameworks for building environments where distractions are minimised, and his purpose can thrive.

From Disempowerment to Empowerment

I once worked at a small startup led by a complex character who was both charismatic and volatile, frequently swinging between tyrannical outbursts and being overly supportive and invested in my growth. He introduced me to many others he'd mentored into successful careers, giving me a false sense of security that I was in good hands. However, his erratic behaviour escalated over time, and without noting, I adjusted my boundaries and became desensitised to it.

Eventually, his mood swings became so extreme that my only other female colleague and I began avoiding the office as much as we could. After one particularly intense period, I had to come in to host a lunch with him aimed at building relationships with business contacts. Knowing his pattern, I joked with my colleague beforehand that I was about to endure an afternoon of 'love-bombing.'

As the lunch progressed, things took a disturbing turn. He drank heavily and, right in the middle of conversations with our guests, began to molest me under the table. I froze, torn between maintaining professionalism and addressing the violation. My mind raced with conflicting thoughts: *I can't make a scene right now—not in front of people we're trying to impress.*

This was a fragile startup, and any disruption could have serious consequences. I was deeply invested in the business, literally on the verge of signing papers to buy shares, and worried about how this incident could impact the company.

At the same time, anxiety gnawed at me over the boundaries he was crossing: *He's my boss! We are supposed to be friends! He would never do this to his male protégés . . .*

Waves of confusion and distress cycled through my mind as I tried to maintain a steady conversation with the clients, caught between my discomfort and the stakes involved. Paralysed and unable to act, I sat there for half an hour, allowing it to happen before finding a break in the conversation to excuse myself and go home.

I immediately told my colleague, who shared my perplexity about how to deal with this situation because the senior stakeholders were his close friends. For a while, I tried to dismiss the whole situation as him being drunk. But a week later, I couldn't shake the unsettled feeling and eventually confided in a trusted male colleague who urged that reporting this incident to leadership was the right thing to do. This gave me the courage to speak up a few days later.

The leadership team responded with sympathy. They said they were becoming increasingly concerned with his bullying in the workplace, noting that he had a tendency to go down self-destructive paths, and this incident would mark their third intervention with him over the years. Their reaction normalised the situation for me, making me feel less guilty for 'ratting him out,' as though my actions were a necessary part of addressing a problem that they had already seen escalating.

However, I was deeply concerned about the ripple effect this would have on others in the business, including him, as they'd mentioned he had suicidal tendencies in previous downward spirals. It felt important to me that whatever action was taken had minimal impact on everyone. I also felt the need to distance myself from this as fast as I could and maintain my privacy. They agreed to honour my request, presenting a watered-down version of the incident involving me and rather focusing more on the episodes reflecting his 'tyrannical' behaviour. This resulted in him losing his position as CEO.

However, when they publicly announced it to the company, they immediately followed it with fifteen minutes of public praise, apparently to soften the impact of his demotion. I couldn't reconcile the various layers of the situation, leaving me feeling strangely disillusioned. However, I didn't realise at the time that I was dissociating.

The turning point came when the only female board member took me aside to hear my version of events directly. As I recounted not just the incident but the broader toxic culture he had created, she was appalled. She admitted this was far more serious than she realised. Initially, she had believed his version of events, where he downplayed his actions and framed the situation as a consensual relationship, but my account revealed a far more serious reality. Determined to address the issue properly, she escalated the matter to a formal investigation, finally giving me a sense of validation and safety that I hadn't realised I needed.

This realisation became a pivotal wake-up call. At the time, I believed the leadership team was acting in good faith, respecting my boundaries while addressing the issue. But in hindsight, their actions were more about maintaining their relationships with him than truly confronting the harm he had done.

It wasn't until the female board member insisted on a formal investigation that the systemic failures at play came to light. Her intervention exposed how privilege, unconscious bias, and fragility had allowed such behaviour to persist unchecked. It also led me to recognise my role in this dynamic: I had relinquished my power and relied on others to act, leaving me vulnerable and unprotected.

Through this experience, I awakened to the shadows of distorted power and boundaries—not just within the system but also within myself. Recognising these patterns gave me the language to understand the dynamics at play internally and externally. With this awareness, I was able to reclaim my power, protect myself more effectively, and better challenge systems of power from a place of integrity and sovereignty.

Taking Purposeful Action

One of the greatest obstacles in Action-Oriented Manifestation is overexertion. This challenge stems from the distorted masculine tendency to relentlessly pursue results, often driven by external pressures to do more. This often leads to burnout, scattered energy, and actions disconnected from true purpose, ultimately stalling manifestation rather than advancing it.

In contrast, the King offers the gift of aligned action, reminding us that less is more. Aligned, intentional steps yield far greater results than the 'hustle' or 'grind' of constantly working harder, taking on more, and pushing forward without ensuring alignment. The King teaches that when action is taken with purpose and precision, each move serves the larger vision and is in harmony with the bigger picture, avoiding the trap of doing more simply for the sake of doing.

By regularly checking in with your inner compass, you can avoid misaligned actions that drain energy. The King also understands the importance of timing—knowing when to act and when to pause. Through this measured approach, energy is conserved and channelled wisely, leading to impactful manifestations grounded in clarity and stability.

> **Eckhart Tolle's *The Power of Now***
>
> In my early journey into personal development, I read *The Power of Now* by Eckhart Tolle while sitting outside in the sun. As I absorbed his words on embracing the present, I felt a profound shift—a stillness I had never fully experienced before. Until then, my focus had always been on the hustle, constantly caught in the pull of 'what's next' with my goals and achievements and filling my schedule with back-to-back plans. But reading Tolle's message on presence, I finally paused, took in my surroundings, and experienced the fullness of the moment.
>
> This sense of grounded presence is deeply aligned with the King archetype, where authentic leadership arises from inner calm and clarity. Tolle's journey reflects this inner mastery. Before becoming a global spiritual teacher, he struggled with a deep existential crisis, grappling with the shadows of identity and ego. At his lowest point, he questioned the very 'I' that was suffering. This self-inquiry led to a profound awakening, guiding him to transcend his ego and embrace a state of presence that would become the foundation of his teachings.

Chapter 8 – The King Archetype: The Powerful Leader

> Like the King archetype, Tolle's path to influence wasn't driven by ambition or a desire to dominate; instead, his work grew organically from a deep alignment within. His writings, lectures, and teachings emerged as natural extensions of his inner peace and clarity, embodying the King's gift of aligned action. For Tolle, it wasn't about a grand plan or a calculated path to success—it was about living in alignment with his truth, and his purpose emerged from there.

Journal Prompts

1. Where does my effort feel like a grind?
   Identify where hard work feels draining rather than fulfilling.

2. What boundaries do I need to establish to protect myself?
   Consider where you may lack boundaries or where overly rigid boundaries might be limiting your growth.

3. What steps am I taking to ensure alignment before acting?
   Consider whether your actions are grounded in strategy and foresight or are reactive and unfocused.

4. What's my relationship with power?
   Consider how you perceive and interact with power in different situations.

5. In which situations do I feel big or small, and why?
   Reflect on how your sense of rank or status shifts in different environments and what this reveals about your inner authority and self-worth.

From King to Magician

The King embodies aligned action, leading with purpose and executing his vision with clarity and poise. The Magician, however, works in the realm of possibilities. His power is not in physical action but in bending reality itself—he manipulates time, bridging the gap between the present and the future, collapsing what once seemed distant into the now.

CHAPTER 9
The Magician Archetype: The Quantum Jumper

"The world as we have created it is a process of our thinking. It cannot be changed without changing our thinking."

—Albert Einstein

THE MAGICIAN HARNESSES the potential of the quantum field to unite vision with reality. Following the King's strategic insight, the Magician blends focused vision with the Lover's embodied resonance, bringing future possibilities into the present and synchronising inner intention with outer manifestation.

In this phase of manifestation, the Magician operates within a realm where all outcomes coexist and can collapse timelines by concentrating on a single, harmonious outcome. By aligning with what is already possible, the Magician draws desired future outcomes into the present, accelerating creation by shifting potential outcomes (possibility) into likely outcomes (probability).

The Magician's energy is one of sharp intention, seamless alignment, and a deep synergy between vision and embodiment. Through mental clarity, visionary insight, and energetic precision, the Magician channels desired realities into form without force, allowing manifestation to feel immediate and real.

Chapter 9 – The Magician Archetype: The Quantum Jumper

Without the Magician's influence, manifestation risks becoming stagnant, leaving dreams to drift in potential rather than progress toward reality. Neglecting his gifts can lead to hesitation or detachment from our deepest desires, causing us to lose the clarity and focus essential for creation. Engaging the Magician, on the other hand, allows us to transcend mere possibility, bringing thought and intention into vibrant, present form with coherence and ease.

GIFTS

Future Embodiment
Aligning his thoughts, actions, and energy to the future self reality he wants to create.

Focused Intent
Harnessing the power of clear, intentional thought and directing energy toward specific goals with purpose.

Clarity
Visionary insight, sees beyond the present, identifying the path to opportunities and innovative solutions.

Quantum Leaping
Rapidly accelerates manifestation by collapsing timelines and bringing the future into the present day reality.

What the mind believes, the world will echo.

Chapter 9 – The Magician Archetype: The Quantum Jumper

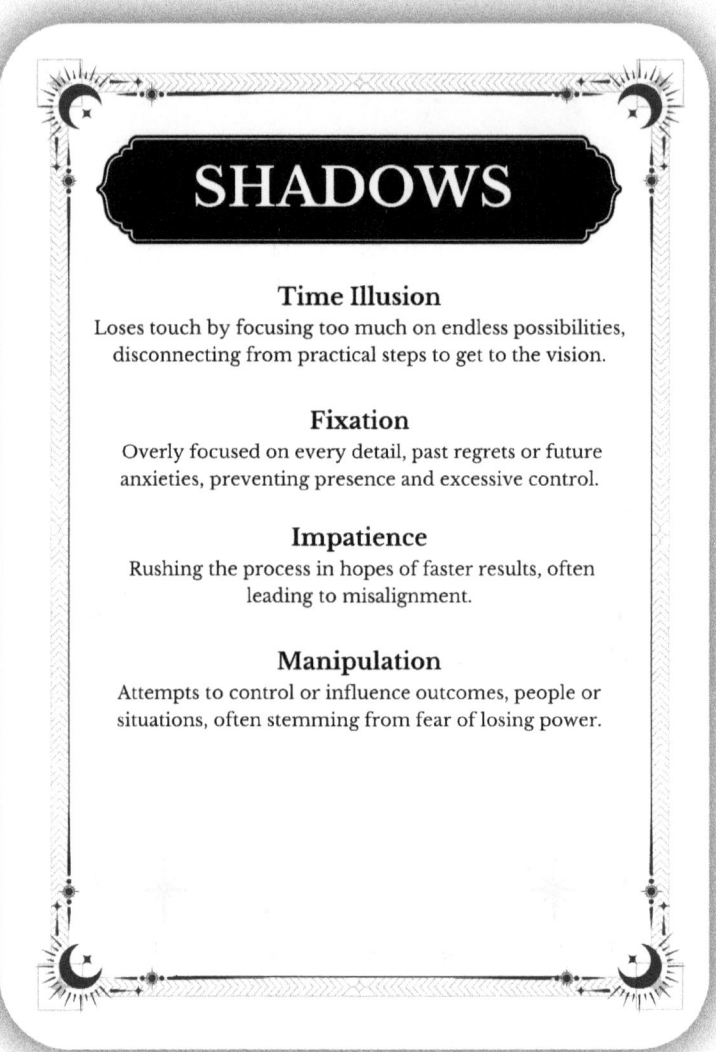

SHADOWS

Time Illusion
Loses touch by focusing too much on endless possibilities, disconnecting from practical steps to get to the vision.

Fixation
Overly focused on every detail, past regrets or future anxieties, preventing presence and excessive control.

Impatience
Rushing the process in hopes of faster results, often leading to misalignment.

Manipulation
Attempts to control or influence outcomes, people or situations, often stemming from fear of losing power.

A magician lost in illusion becomes the trick he plays.

Overcoming the Obstacles of the Magician

The Magician's greatest challenge is trusting his ability to bring ideas and visions to life. When he doubts and second-guesses himself, he hesitates and misses opportunities. To overcome this, the Magician must let go of the need for certainty and believe in his ability to harness the future into the present moment.

Embodying the Self-Fulfilling Prophecy

A common obstacle for the Magician is **deferred identity**, a tendency to fixate on the idea that fulfilment only comes once a specific destination or goal is reached. This belief stems from illusions that separate us from our desired state, leading to cycles of waiting and unfulfillment. Thoughts like, *I'll be wealthy once I save this money*, or *I'll be fulfilled when I have more time*, place excessive focus on external markers, and impose a rigid view of time, reinforcing the belief that the present is insufficient.

This disconnect traps us in linear thinking, deferring fulfilment to the future instead of embracing it in the present.

> *"When you change within, so does the world around you. When you realise that all of time exists in the present moment, you unlock the magic of creation. The future and past are but echoes of the now. Time does not create; it only reveals."*

The Law of Resonance reminds us that our inner state shapes our external world. Even if our surroundings don't yet reflect our aspirations, we can begin embodying the energy of our future selves now. By doing so, we create a self-fulfilling prophecy, naturally drawing opportunities and experiences that align with our vision.

Chapter 9 – The Magician Archetype: The Quantum Jumper

> **Chris Hadfield's *Becoming His Future Self***
>
> A powerful case study on the Law of Resonance is astronaut Chris Hadfield. Inspired by the Apollo 11 Moon landing at age nine, Hadfield made a lifelong commitment to becoming an astronaut. He began thinking and behaving like one, asking himself daily, *What would an astronaut do?*
>
> This question guided his actions: he joined the Air Cadets as a teenager, earned his pilot license by 16, excelled in engineering studies, and trained rigorously in aviation and survival skills. By embodying his future self daily, he dissolved the illusion of separation between his vision and reality. By the time his dream materialised, he had already been living that reality for years. This is the Magician's approach: aligning with the energy of the future self to allow manifestation to flow effortlessly.

Focusing Intent to Collapse Aligned Timelines

The Magician understands that time is an illusion where past, present, and future coexist. This aligns with the principle of superposition, where multiple realities exist simultaneously. Rather than trying to control every step, the Magician channels focused intent on the desired outcome, visualising it with clarity and full belief. This unwavering focus— free from doubt, excessive control, or manipulation—allows the Magician to collapse multiple possibilities into the reality he seeks, naturally aligned with his vision.

However, obstacles can disrupt this flow. When we fixate on every detail, as seen in the Maiden, we risk becoming trapped in the 'how,' over-analysing each step towards our desired outcome. This intense focus can create mental barriers, ultimately hindering manifestation by disrupting the natural flow needed to collapse timelines. By getting caught up in details, second-guessing every decision, and fearing deviation from a specific plan, we delay action and fuel doubt, preventing us from moving forward with confidence.

At the other extreme, an abundance of future possibilities can overwhelm us, leading to scattered energy. With so many pathways, confusion sets in, making it difficult to discern which path most aligns with our vision. This overwhelm prevents clear decision-making and can keep us stuck in indecision.

Lastly, the power of visionary insight can be misused to manipulate situations or people by leveraging a heightened ability to assess dynamics and predict outcomes. This might involve anticipating others' vulnerabilities, steering decisions to gain an unfair advantage, or using foresight to control outcomes. Such behaviour disrupts trust and creates resistance, prioritising scarcity and control over the energy of abundance, which thrives on openness, reciprocity, and shared growth.

Aligning with Heart and Mind with Visionary Insight

When the Magician overthinks, he remains stuck outside the present, caught in cycles of past regrets or anxieties about the future. This mental loop not only triggers stress and anxiety but also disrupts our ability to manifest by holding us in timelines that prevent focused, intentional creation. To manifest effectively, the Magician needs a clear vision of the Maiden's dream—and to tap into the future beyond that dream—unclouded by distraction or doubt.

The key to collapsing timelines is not only envisioning the outcome but also aligning them with the powerful emotions of the Lover: love, joy, and gratitude. When we feel these emotions in the present, they bridge the gap between 'someday' and 'now,' making the vision feel accessible and real. This creates a coherent state where the mind and heart align, amplifying our intentions and moving us closer to our desires.

When heart and mind align, the Magician brings distant possibilities into the present, collapsing timelines and inviting synchronicity. Attuned to the moment, he transforms intention into reality, allowing manifestation to unfold with purpose and ease.

Chapter 9 – The Magician Archetype: The Quantum Jumper

> **HeartMath Institute** *Harnessing Heart Coherence*
>
> The HeartMath Institute's research delves into the transformative state of 'heart coherence,' where the heart, mind, and emotions work together in harmony. This state not only fosters mental clarity and emotional balance but also enhances our ability to manifest by aligning inner and outer energies. Key benefits of heart coherence include:
>
> - Synchronising bodily responses and brainwave patterns to promote calm and empowerment.
>
> - Aligns intentions with emotional and physical equilibrium, enhancing goal achievement and decision-making.
>
> - Expands the heart's electromagnetic field, strengthening connections with others and influencing the surrounding environment.
>
> - Reduces inner stress and resistance, amplifying the effectiveness of intentions and visualisations.
>
> - Increases synchronicities, which help align our intentions with the right opportunities, making it easier to achieve our goals.

Co-Creation with the Quantum Field

A core obstacle for the Magician is the illusion of control over the quantum field, assuming he can direct every outcome by sheer intention. While the Magician's connection to this realm is powerful, this attachment to control creates resistance, as he becomes overly fixated on specific outcomes rather than allowing manifestation to unfold organically.

This control-driven mindset leads the Magician to believe he can predict or force how desires should materialise. In doing so, he loses touch with the fluid and boundless nature of the quantum field, inadvertently limiting its potential. By gripping too tightly to a single vision, he restricts the field's potential, blocking alternative outcomes that might better serve his journey.

This is where the final archetype, the Sage, complements and balances out the Magician, introducing the wisdom of detachment. Through the Sage's influence, the Magician learns to shift from controlling to *harmonising* with the quantum field's vast potential. This subtle detachment allows him to hold his vision lightly, treating the quantum field as a co-creative partner rather than something to be directed.

In embracing this balance, the Magician moves beyond the illusion of control, manifesting with greater fluidity and trust. By releasing fixated expectations, he opens himself to the universe's wisdom, allowing it to shape outcomes in ways that align seamlessly with his energy and purpose.

> **Burt Goldman's** *Quantum Jumping Transformation*
>
> Burt Goldman, known as *The American Monk*, exemplified the *Magician* archetype through his pioneering work in **Quantum Jumping**. In his 80s, Goldman sought to explore new talents he had never pursued before—such as painting, photography, and music. Using his unique Quantum Jumping technique, Goldman meditated and visualised himself accessing alternate versions of himself in parallel universes—versions that had already mastered his desired skills.
>
> Goldman had previously built a successful career as an instructor of the Silva Method, a mind development and manifestation technique. As he aged, he felt compelled to continue evolving, leading him to experiment with alternate realities. By 'jumping' into these parallel selves, he rapidly acquired new skills.

> Within a short time, Goldman became a renowned painter and photographer, with his art displayed in galleries worldwide. His journey wasn't just about developing new talents; it highlighted the limitless potential of the quantum field. By trusting the process, Goldman avoided common pitfalls like over-control and impatience, which often disrupt manifestation. He emphasised the importance of aligning thoughts and emotions with a desired future, allowing the quantum field to bring that vision into reality.
>
> Goldman's journey demonstrates that transformation is possible at any age. Through quantum leaping, individuals can create extraordinary shifts in their lives. His journey serves as a powerful reminder that mastery and self-evolution are achievable when one trusts the process and embraces the potential of the quantum field.

Journal Prompts

1. How can I simplify my approach to avoid overcomplicating and perfectionism?
   Consider strategies to release control over details and stay focused on your desired outcomes.

2. How can I trust the destination without becoming distracted by obsessing over the path to get there?
   Reflect on every doubt or question about the "how" that comes to mind so you can release them and refocus on your vision.

3. Where can I embody the qualities of my future self today?
   Identify actions that align you with the energy of the person you aspire to become.

4. How do I perceive time in relation to my goals?
   Reflect on any rigidity around timelines and consider how flexibility could allow unexpected opportunities.

5. What vision does my future self – who has already achieved my goals – see for me next?
Imagine the aspirations that arise once your current goals are fulfilled.

From Magician to Sage

While the Magician teaches us that we can accelerate manifestation with focus and intention, the Sage reminds us of detachment and patience. As the final archetype, we learn that there is no separation at all, and everything unfolds perfectly in divine timing.

CHAPTER 10
The Sage Archetype: The Universal Guide

"The universe is not outside of you. Look inside yourself; everything that you want, you already are."

—*Rumi*

THE SAGE EMBODIES the final and most refined step in manifestation, where intentional effort gives way to a profound unity with all that is. After journeying through the previous archetypes and gathering insights, the Sage invites us to quiet the mind, embrace pure awareness, and allow wisdom beyond action to take root.

In this ultimate phase, manifestation becomes less about individual desires and more about resonating with the field of *pure potentiality*. Here, all possibilities coexist within the quantum field and are accessible not through striving but by resting in oneness. There is no separation between self and universe; in this state, manifestation arises naturally, emerging from alignment with a boundless consciousness.

The Sage brings an energy of profound stillness, humility, and acceptance of life's paradoxes. With a timeless perspective and ease, he allows manifestations to unfold without interference, trusting fully in the universe's flow. By releasing attachment and control, the Sage opens us to subtle synchronicities and quiet guidance, sensing the universe's gentle hand within each moment.

When we neglect the Sage's influence, we risk becoming entangled in the mind's need for control and intellect, distanced from the expansive field of universal insight. This disconnection creates strain and makes manifestation feel forced. Embracing the Sage, we find quiet confidence in life's rhythm, experiencing manifestation as a seamless, powerful process grounded in unity.

The Inside Players: Master the Manifestation Game

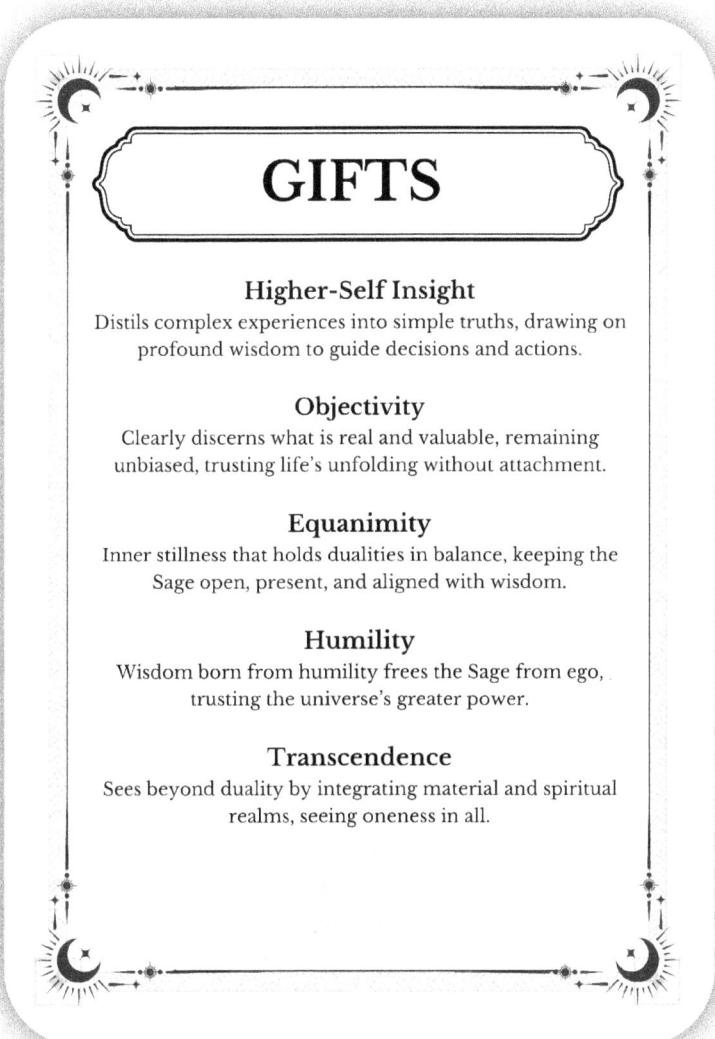

GIFTS

Higher-Self Insight
Distils complex experiences into simple truths, drawing on profound wisdom to guide decisions and actions.

Objectivity
Clearly discerns what is real and valuable, remaining unbiased, trusting life's unfolding without attachment.

Equanimity
Inner stillness that holds dualities in balance, keeping the Sage open, present, and aligned with wisdom.

Humility
Wisdom born from humility frees the Sage from ego, trusting the universe's greater power.

Transcendence
Sees beyond duality by integrating material and spiritual realms, seeing oneness in all.

He listens to the silence, for wisdom speaks between the lines of knowing.

Chapter 10 – The Sage Archetype: The Universal Guide

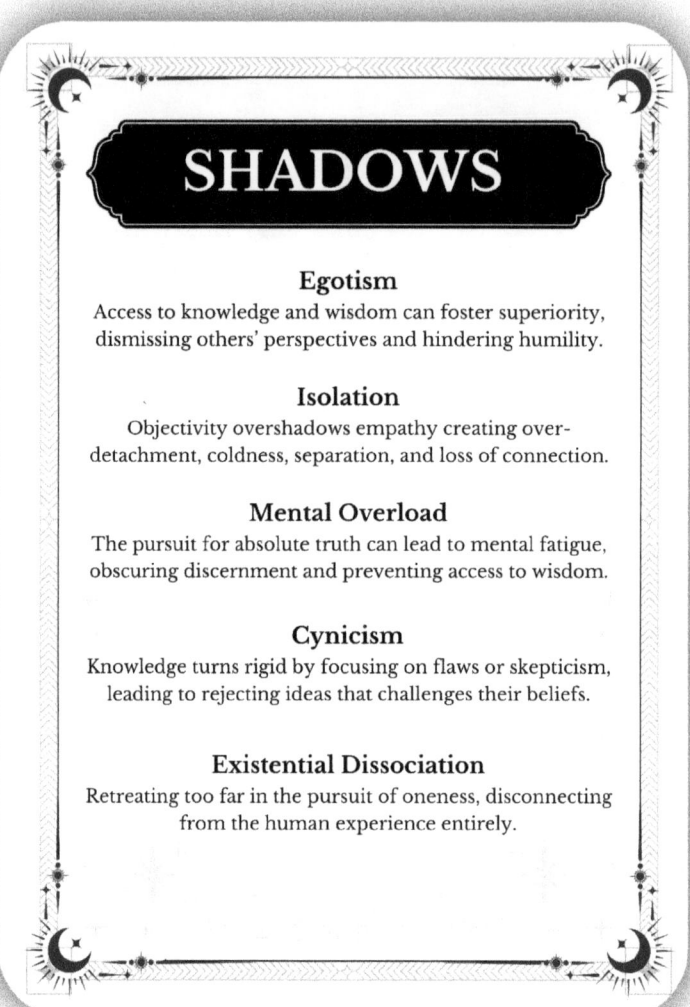

SHADOWS

Egotism
Access to knowledge and wisdom can foster superiority, dismissing others' perspectives and hindering humility.

Isolation
Objectivity overshadows empathy creating over-detachment, coldness, separation, and loss of connection.

Mental Overload
The pursuit for absolute truth can lead to mental fatigue, obscuring discernment and preventing access to wisdom.

Cynicism
Knowledge turns rigid by focusing on flaws or skepticism, leading to rejecting ideas that challenges their beliefs.

Existential Dissociation
Retreating too far in the pursuit of oneness, disconnecting from the human experience entirely.

A mind too full of answers has no space for wisdom.

Overcoming the Obstacles of the Sage

The Sage's obstacles stem from an overactive ego and a relentless pursuit for answers, which clouds intuition and creates resistance, making it challenging to recognise new possibilities or opportunities. To overcome this, the Sage must quiet the mind, detach from ego-driven thoughts, and trust their inner wisdom, leading to greater alignment with their goals.

Cultivating Deep Humility

A central obstacle for the Sage archetype is attachment to the ego, which often manifests as a desire to stand out as uniquely wise. This attachment fosters separation and superiority, creating barriers to humility and the interconnectedness necessary for accessing deeper wisdom. When the ego prioritises distinction over unity, it can dismiss valuable perspectives, limiting growth and insight.

The ego's attachment to outcomes and identity-based validation also fuels resistance in the manifestation process. Driven by insecurity, it clings tightly to control, fearing irrelevance without recognition. This fixation disrupts the clarity required for surrender and blocks the Sage from tapping into the flow of divine timing.

> *"We must learn to observe the ego with humility, recognising that our true essence lies beyond ego-based narratives."*

By adopting humility, the Sage transcends ego-driven illusion and reconnects with the higher self. This alignment allows wisdom to flow from unity rather than separation, liberating the Sage from identity-driven desires. In this state, manifestation unfolds naturally, guided by the universe's inherent wisdom.

Chapter 10 – The Sage Archetype: The Universal Guide

Developing Detached Trust

This deep humility is where the **Law of Detachment** comes into play. It invites us to release our attachment to specific outcomes, trusting that life will unfold in ways that ultimately align with our growth and well-being. Non-attachment does not mean we stop caring about our desires; rather, it involves letting go of the need to control every detail.

For the Sage, embodying this wisdom means recognising that, just like planting a seed, we don't need to dig it up each day to check its progress. We trust that, with the right conditions, it will bloom in its own time.

> **Hakuin Ekaku's** *Wisdom of Detachment*
>
> A well-known Zen story beautifully illustrates the power of detachment. Hakuin Ekaku, a revered Zen master, was known for his wisdom and calm nature. One day, a young woman in the village became pregnant and, in distress, falsely accused Hakuin of being the father. Her parents confronted Hakuin, berating him and demanding that he take responsibility for the child.
>
> Without protest or defence, Hakuin simply replied, "Is that so?" and accepted the child into his care.
>
> For years, Hakuin raised the child with love and tenderness, even as his reputation was ruined. Villagers and disciples alike expressed shock and disappointment, yet Hakuin showed no anger or resistance—only peaceful acceptance. A year later, the young woman confessed that the real father was a man from the fish market. Her parents returned to Hakuin, apologised profusely, and asked for the child back.
>
> Once again, without resentment, Hakuin handed over the child, simply saying, "Is that so?"

The Inside Players: Master the Manifestation Game

> This story demonstrates the power of non-attachment. Hakuin's response—"Is that so?"— reflects his ability to face life's challenges without becoming attached to specific outcomes or judgements. He surrendered control over how others perceived him, allowing life to unfold as it would, meeting every moment with acceptance.
>
> Hakuin's story encapsulates the Sage's approach to the Law of Detachment. Non-attachment is not indifference; it is a profound trust in the flow of life, knowing that by releasing control, everything falls into place in its perfect time and way.

However, while detached trust exemplifies profound surrender to life's flow, taken to the extreme, this detachment can lead to isolation. When the Sage's pursuit of objectivity becomes excessive, it risks creating a wall of disconnection—replacing empathy with cold detachment and turning peace into distance.

Rather than enhancing connection, extreme detachment can lead to a sense of separation from others and from a grounding in the material world. The balance is found by mastering the art of equanimity, learning to balance detachment with grounded presence, and engaging deeply with both the spiritual and earthly realms, thereby holding space for both unity and personal experience.

Accessing Higher-Self Wisdom with a Quiet Mind

Ego attachment often traps people in mental overload, relying too heavily on intellect and rationalising every outcome. This need for mental control creates noise, clouding the ability to access higher wisdom. Obsessing over every detail leads to inner turbulence and anxiety, which obscures clarity and triggers **analysis paralysis,** where the fear of uncertainty prevents forward movement. When we are consumed by mental chatter, we become disconnected from our higher-self insights.

Alternatively, when we learn to quiet the mind and balance intellect with stillness, we release the need for certainty and become open to subtle signals like synchronicities, enabling manifestation to flow naturally.

Remaining Objective in Conflict

Overexposure to many hard truths can lead to a hardening that creates a jaded cynicism, like a weathered soul who has seen too much go wrong to expect anything to go right. This loss of faith—much like someone who has lost faith in humanity—turns into a shield, a self-protective mechanism that keeps vulnerability at bay.

Over time, this guarded scepticism hardens into a rigid worldview, where the Sage, wary of past disappointments, instinctively dismisses new ideas or unfamiliar paths. Unlike the Maiden's open curiosity, this jaded outlook sees the unknown as a threat, inhibiting the insight and intuitive flow needed for manifestation to unfold naturally.

By cultivating objectivity through a neutral, observational stance, we can learn to see success and failure as interconnected aspects of a larger journey. Through this neutrality, we release the ego's need for control and certainty, breaking free from the chains of scepticism. Embracing an open, unbiased mindset clears mental space for new possibilities, allowing insight and inspiration to flow naturally.

Attuning to Oneness

As we discussed, when the Sage's pursuit of oneness goes too far, it can lead to a disconnection from reality. However, in a state of balance, the Sage embodies profound unity, perceiving no division between the self and the universe, the inner and outer worlds, or the unmanifested and the manifested.

While the Magician taps into the quantum field to shape outcomes, the Sage takes this understanding further, dissolving distinctions entirely to align fully with life's flow. This concept mirrors **quantum**

entanglement, where once-connected particles remain intertwined regardless of the perceived distance between them.

For the Sage, life itself is a similar web, with each intention and experience woven into a unified field of existence.

> *"In this state, all possibilities coexist, ready to emerge naturally through alignment with universal intelligence."*

In this state of oneness, the Sage neither directs nor controls outcomes but trusts the unfolding of all possibilities in alignment with universal intelligence. Moving us beyond struggle, the Sage accesses a field of infinite potential, allowing desires to manifest effortlessly as part of this seamless unity.

The Unfolding of Divine Timing

Divine timing is a natural extension of the Sage's wisdom of oneness. Here, timing isn't external or something to control; it is a rhythm intrinsic to the universe's flow. Divine timing aligns with the Sage's acceptance that each event, opportunity, and connection unfolds precisely when resonance is aligned. This awareness fosters patience and surrender, allowing the Sage to release urgency and control, confident that what resonates with their energy will manifest at the right moment.

Unlike forceful, action-driven approaches, the Sage trusts that each experience arrives at its own perfect time. This trust cultivates a sense of ease, freeing the Sage from anxiety or impatience, entering a state of relaxed confidence where manifestation flows harmoniously with life's rhythm. Through this perspective, the Sage becomes an energetic match for their desires, inviting them to unfold naturally.

Chapter 10 – The Sage Archetype: The Universal Guide

The Magic of Synchronicities

Synchronicities are meaningful coincidences that affirm the Sage's alignment with life's greater flow. Introduced by Carl Jung as connections emerging from the collective unconscious, synchronicities appear to the Sage as purposeful signs from the universe. These experiences—such as encountering a helpful message repeatedly or meeting someone precisely when needed—act as gentle confirmations that they are attuned to life's underlying symphony.

For the Sage, synchronicities are woven into the fabric of oneness, reflecting moments where inner and outer worlds resonate. Observing these signs with calm appreciation, light amusement, and detachment, the Sage deepens their trust in the unseen order, feeling a sense of belonging within the universal flow. This relaxed attentiveness allows insights to arise naturally, unfiltered by intellect or ego. It reinforces the Sage's openness to life's unfolding.

Without this trust in oneness, divine timing, and synchronicity, the Sage risks becoming entangled in the mind's limitations, clinging to control and relying solely on logic. This disconnection obstructs universal guidance, leaving them confined to the intellect alone. Embracing these principles, the Sage cultivates quiet confidence, knowing that manifestations arrive in alignment with a higher order. Manifestation is no longer about effort but about resonance, with desires emerging naturally from a place of inner harmony.

> **From Micromanaging to Co-Creation**
>
> Even after cultivating a daily lifestyle centred on surrendered manifestation, pregnancy offered a profound opportunity to deepen my relationship with trust. The level of uncertainty it brought was expected, but the timing caught me off guard. I thought we'd have more time to prepare. Yet, suddenly, I felt immense pressure to ensure we had enough savings for my maternity leave. Old habits crept back—overthinking, planning every detail, and slipping into hustle mode. Each day

that brought us closer to the birth heightened my worry and desire to control the situation.

One particularly overwhelming day, I arrived for an acupuncture session feeling frantic. My acupuncturist immediately sensed my energy and gently reminded me of something simple yet powerful: my body was already doing so much by creating life, and I needed to slow down. She encouraged me to shift out of constant action and into receptivity. "The universe is here to support you," she said, "but you must ask for it. Set an intention for the support you need and trust it will come effortlessly."

This message was the synchronistic reminder I needed to realise I was holding on too tightly to the details, leaving no room for the universe to work its magic. From that moment, I made a conscious shift. Each morning, I set an intention—not just for the desired outcomes but for them to unfold with ease and grace. I asked for synchronicities to guide me and trusted that the answers would arrive in divine timing. Instead of trying to solve the uncertainty, I allowed myself to sit with it, leaning into stillness and receptivity through meditation.

The results were nothing short of miraculous. As I released control, synchronicities began to flow. Clients reached out unexpectedly, unplanned opportunities materialised, and support arrived exactly when I needed it. What had once felt like overwhelming uncertainty transformed into a series of perfectly timed events that I couldn't have orchestrated myself.

This experience anchored me in a deeper surrender. I no longer felt the need to force outcomes or anxiously anticipate the next step. Trust became my foundation, and everything worked out far better than I could have imagined. It reaffirmed a profound truth: when we create space for the universe to co-create with us, it meets us where we are, often exceeding our expectations.

Surrender isn't a one-time act—it's a practice, an ongoing invitation to trust life's unfolding. As I embraced this lesson, I felt more present and grounded than ever before. Life doesn't always go according to our plans, but when we let go, it often unfolds in ways far greater than we could have dreamed.

Journal Prompts

1. When does my search for answers lead to mental overload instead of clarity?
   Reflect on moments where overanalysis has left you stuck in a cycle of overthinking, disconnecting you from intuition.

2. How does my ego influence my actions?
   Notice signs that show when ego, rather than intuition, is guiding you.

3. When has pride or the need to be 'right' gotten in the way of my learning or growth?
   Reflect on whether attachment to being 'correct' has limited your ability to learn from others or explore new perspectives.

4. What synchronicities have I experienced, and what was my attitude towards it at the time?
   Recall these meaningful signs and explore ways to stay open to their guidance.

5. When have I mistaken intellectual superiority for wisdom?
   Reflect on whether your knowledge has ever led to dismissiveness or a lack of receptivity to the perspectives of others.

The Sage leaves us with the understanding that true manifestation blends intention, trust, and divine timing. Through patience and releasing control, we align with life's infinite possibilities, becoming a transmission of our desires without the need to chase or force outcomes.

Surrendering allows us to align effortlessly with the possibilities around us, embodying both the creator and the creation.

As you continue your journey, remember that everything you desire is already within reach. Trust the timing of the universe and surrender to its flow, knowing that what is meant for you is on its way.

CHAPTER 11
Manifestation Practices

"What you seek is seeking you."

—*Rumi*

As we progress on our journey, conscious manifestation becomes less about theory and more about grounded, daily practices to get yourself into a *state of being*. Integrating simple yet powerful actions into your routine creates a steady foundation on which your intentions can unfold.

Each step is designed to align your mind, body, and spirit with the flow of manifestation, setting you up to receive fully. As you align with your deepest desires, the universe, in turn, aligns with you, bringing what you seek into your life with ease.

Setting Up Your Day

Morning is a powerful time for setting intentions. Each day offers a fresh slate, a chance to realign with your highest goals. By setting a morning intention, you shape the energy you carry through your day, aligning your thoughts, emotions, and actions with your dreams.

Step 1: Energy Clearing and Protection

Begin each day by clearing your energy and creating a protective barrier. Sit comfortably, close your eyes, and take a deep breath. As you exhale, visualise a golden light surrounding you, forming a protective shield. Instruct any thoughts, emotions, or external influences that don't serve you to dissolve into this light, leaving you feeling refreshed and aligned.

Step 2: Grounding Breathwork

Anchor yourself in the present moment through breathwork. Inhale slowly for a count of four, hold for four, and exhale for four. Repeat this 'box breathing' cycle three times, feeling your body relax. Imagine drawing in fresh energy with each inhale and releasing tension with each exhale, grounding yourself for the day ahead.

Step 3: Set Your Daily Intention

With your energy cleared, visualise how you'd like your day to unfold. Picture yourself moving through your tasks of the day with ease, meeting supportive people, and encountering and being receptive to synchronicities that align with your goals. Consider questions like:

- How would you like each event to unfold?
- What do you wish to experience or achieve?
- What would you like to release or invite more of?

Invite guidance in the form of creativity, inspiring breakthroughs, helpful connections, solutions, or symbols that affirm your journey.

Step 4: Anchoring the Intention

Visualise your intention as an object, such as a key, stone, or flower symbolising your desires. Hold this object in your heart space, take a deep breath, and as you exhale, let it merge into your heart. Feel the energy of your intention integrating within you. Spend a moment inviting the highest request of love, gratitude, and receptivity, then surrender into a deep knowing that everything is aligning in your favour.

Step 5: Daily Check-Ins and Regulation

Throughout your day, take a few moments to check in with yourself. Notice how you're feeling: Are you aligned with the intention you set in the morning? Are you observing any synchronicities or supportive encounters? If at any point you feel off-balance or tense, pause, take a few deep breaths to recentre, and realign with your intention. Use the following simple techniques to bring yourself back into a state of calm and regulation.

<u>Sound Vibration Techniques</u>

- **Humming:** Humming creates a gentle vibration in the chest and throat, stimulating the vagus nerve and promoting relaxation. Humming softly for a few moments helps ground you and ease tension.choosing a personal mantra—one that resonates deeply with your intentions or values— can make the practice even more meaningful. Allow the sound to resonate in your chest and throat, calming the nervous system and helping you feel more centred.
- **Calming Mantra:** Repeat the mantra "I am safe, I am grounded" as you take deep belly breaths. Inhale deeply through your nose, expanding your belly, and exhale slowly through your mouth. This affirmation and breath combination helps calm your system and reaffirms a sense of stability.

<u>Breathwork</u>

- **Deep Sighing:** Take a deep breath in through your nose, then release it with a long, audible sigh through your mouth. This helps release tension quickly and activates the parasympathetic response. Repeat two to three times for an immediate calming effect.
- **4-7-8 Breathing:** Inhale deeply through your nose for a count of four, hold the breath for seven, and exhale slowly through your mouth for eight counts. This technique calms the nervous system and slows the heart rate, inducing a relaxed state.

- **Box Breathing:** Inhale for a count of four, hold the breath for four, exhale for four, and hold again for four. Repeat this 'box' cycle several times to centre your focus and calm your mind and body.

Hands-On Grounding Techniques

- **Ear Massage:** Begin with an ear massage to gently activate the vagus nerve and release initial tension. Massage from the tops of your ears down to the earlobes, using slow, circular motions for 15–20 seconds. This is a subtle, calming start to the grounding process.
- **Heart and Head Hold:** Place one hand on the back of your head and the other over your heart. This comforting position helps you feel grounded and secure, signalling safety to your body. Pair this with slow, deep breathing to deepen the calming effect.
- **Gentle Eye Pressure:** Lightly place your palms over your closed eyes, applying gentle pressure for 30 seconds to a minute while breathing deeply. This stimulates the vagus nerve and promotes relaxation, making it an ideal next step after the head and heart hold.
- **Tapping with Humming:** As you hum softly, gently tap along your collarbone, chest, or the outer edge of your hands. The combination of sound and tapping on acupressure points along the meridian system releases tension and helps ground you further.
- **Felt-Sense Grounding:** Stand or sit comfortably and notice the sensations of the air around you—the temperature and feeling against your skin. With each exhale, release any stress into the earth, and welcome peace and stability with each inhale. This fully grounds you in the present, enhancing your sense of calm.
- **Cold Water Splash:** End with a cold-water splash on your face or a cool, damp cloth on your forehead. This energising technique activates the body's 'diving reflex,' slowing the heart rate and triggering a quick, refreshing calm.

Step 6: End-of-Day Reflection

Before bed, take a few moments to reflect on your day with gratitude. Recognise any progress, synchronicities, or supportive encounters that align with your intentions.

Consider these questions:

- What synchronicities did I notice?
- How did I move closer to my goals?
- What felt aligned, and what did not?
- Did my actions support my long-term vision?
- What drained my energy, and where could I set more boundaries?

This quick reflection helps you track progress and identify where adjustments are needed. Aim to release any lingering stress, closing your day with heart-centred gratitude and a sense of alignment for tomorrow.

Trust in Imperfection

Remember, not every day will go as planned, and that's perfectly okay. Trust that the universe always aligns events to serve your highest good, even when the path seems uncertain. By committing to this daily manifestation practice, you build a lifestyle that nurtures your deepest desires. Each small, consistent step strengthens the foundation for your future reality, drawing you closer to where you want to be. Begin each day with mindfulness and clarity, anchoring yourself in alignment with your highest self, and allow your manifestations to unfold naturally.

Putting it all Together: Embodying Surrendered Manifestation

> *"Be water, my friend. Water is fluid, soft, and yielding. But water will wear away rock, which is rigid and cannot yield. Be water, my friend, and go with the flow of life, trusting that the universe will guide you when you allow yourself to be fluid and open. Surrender to the process, and like water, you will find your way around every obstacle."*
>
> —*Bruce Lee*

AT THE CORE of manifestation lies a profound truth: we create our reality from the inside out. The journey through these archetypes reveals that manifestation is less about effort and more about aligning with our inner state and trusting the universe to reciprocate. This is a journey of being, not merely doing.

Each archetype has offered unique wisdom. **The Maiden** awakens us to dreams without limits; **the Lover** infuses those dreams with passion and presence; **the Mother** creates a sacred container to hold our desires; **the Huntress** clears any resistance; **the Healer** transforms limitations into empowering beliefs; **the Queen** reclaims our worthiness to receive; and **the Wild Woman** reconnects us with our most authentic truth. Together, these Sacred Feminine energies build a foundation of inner alignment, making space for true abundance to flow.

Once our inner work is complete, our actions will organically flow through the Sacred Masculine. **The King** channels sovereign power into aligned action; **the Magician** collapses timelines, accelerating the manifestation process; and **the Sage** embodies the wisdom of oneness, reminding us that we are inseparable from the universe's infinite unfolding. These masculine energies help us act with certainty, knowing our intentions are already woven into the fabric of existence.

This balance of surrender and action reflects the ancient Taoist concept of **Wu Wei**—effortless action. Wu Wei teaches that when we stop trying to control outcomes, like water, we flow naturally with life, knowing that everything is unfolding as it should. Surrendered manifestation is about releasing the urge to push and accept our reality as a culmination of past actions and choices—an empowering recognition that *we* hold the innate power to consciously create our reality in this moment.

As we progress on our journey, we will encounter unexpected bumps in the road, like the inner critic whispering that we're not moving fast enough or comparing us to others. Sometimes, it may feel like we are swimming upstream, caught in the currents of doubt and pressure. Yet, this is the ebb and flow of life. When we surrender to the understanding that life is occurring exactly as it should, we move with the current with greater ease, trusting that the universe is carrying us where we need to be.

To manifest effortlessly, we must first accept our current reality as it is, without judgement. This acceptance isn't about assigning blame for our circumstances. We may not have caused every aspect of it, but we can recognise that we have the responsibility and power within ourselves to create change *today*.

This acceptance also, of course, doesn't mean abandoning our dreams. Instead, it invites us to release the need for rigid timelines and trust the unfolding of divine timing. Wu Wei reminds us that as we stop struggling, the universe aligns with us. By letting go of control, we align with life's rhythm, moving with its flow rather than against it.

As each archetype has shown, manifestation is less about doing more and more about being aligned with our true desires. The universe responds to our inner state, reflecting our intentions back to us in perfect time. When we release the need to force and allow life to flow, we create space for our desires. The most profound manifestations arise when we trust this flow, stop swimming against the current, and let it carry us so that everything we seek arrives with ease.

So, as you move forward, remember that the key to manifestation is balance. Honour the dance between action and surrender. Accept where you are, release the pressure to make things happen, and trust that your path is unfolding as it should. Let go of resistance, quiet the inner critic, and allow life to carry you toward your dreams.

May you walk this path of the Sacred Feminine Manifestation Method with trust, ease, and balance, knowing that all you desire is already within, waiting to unfold.

Surrender and witness your dreams manifest with grace.

Stay Connected

If you'd like to dive deeper into the themes of this book or explore how manifestation can transform your life, visit my website at www.rachelchristensenofficial.com. There, you can subscribe to my newsletter for bonus resources, meditations, and updates on future offerings.

For more inspiration and insights, follow me on Instagram at @thespiritmagician.

Share Your Journey!
1. I'd love to see how The Inside Players has resonated with you!
2. Snap a photo of the book or your favourite passage.
3. Share it on Instagram and tell me what stood out for you.

Tag me @thespiritmagician and tag **#TheInsidePlayers** so I can celebrate your insights with you! Your post might even be featured on my page! Thank you for being part of this journey.

If this book has inspired you, I'd deeply appreciate it if you could leave a review. Reviews play a crucial role in helping others discover the book. You're also welcome to share your thoughts directly with me through my website or recommend the book to your friends, family, or community.

Your support means so much and helps these ideas reach those who need them most.

Let's continue this journey of growth, alignment, and transformation together.

www.ingramcontent.com/pod-product-compliance
Lightning Source LLC
Chambersburg PA
CBHW062049290426
44109CB00027B/2775